Praise for Carl Jung, Hauntings, and Paranormal Coincidences

"This book is a part of all of us. The journey that we are all taking is inherently connected to those stories told in this book, written with so much joy, curiosity, and intelligence …"

Steven Ballou, Psychotherapist and Adjunct Faculty/ Psychology, Southern New Hampshire University

"Wow! As an experienced and seasoned paranormal investigator (24 years), I really loved this book!"

Jill Borter, Operations Manager and Electronic Voice Phenomena Analyst, Orlando Paranormal Investigations

"Doug Dillon's work helps one better appreciate the magnificence of all that surrounds and defines our existence."

Jim Caccavo, former NEWSWEEK, Vietnam war correspondent/photographer

"What a journey. What a litany of experiences. If you like 'the Paranormal', you'll love *Carl Jung, Hauntings and Paranormal Coincidences*."

Chuck Dowling, Author of The Hammer of God Series, the Story of Arthur

Carl Jung, Hauntings, and Paranormal Coincidences

By

Doug Dillon

Old St. Augustine Publications
Altamonte Springs, Florida
www.oldstaugustinepublications.com

© 2015
By Douglas Dillon

ISBN 978-0-692-38918-8

More books by Doug Dillon from Old St. Augustine Publications

Adult Nonfiction

An Explosion of Being:
An American Family's Journey into the Psychic

Young Adult Fiction

Sliding Beneath the Surface:
The St. Augustine Trilogy, Book I

Stepping Off a Cliff:
The St. Augustine Trilogy, Book II

Targeting Orion's Children:
The St. Augustine Trilogy, Book III

*To All Those
Who Seek Understanding
about the Nature of Our Beings*

Foreword

It is fascinating to me that Doug Dillon had no idea, when he asked me to write the foreword to this book, that I had actually written a paper on Carl Jung when I was in college. That coincidence was amazing enough, but when I began reading his book and discovered that the first incident Doug relates from Dr. Jung's life is the same incident I wrote about in my college paper, I knew that true synchronicity was in place! Coincidence? The odds of that happening are staggering!

This writing is truly a gift from Doug's heart. The intimate revelations about the paranormal happenings in his own life, combined with the paranormal occurrences in Dr. Jung's life, and others, immediately stimulate the curiosity of the reader. How could this happen? Is there a thread in the universe that ties these phenomena together?

Doug unites these events simply by their juxtaposition. So many of us would not have paid attention to such episodes, but what got Doug's attention, and kept it, was the sheer lack of explanation as to how such situations could occur. The beauty of sifting through so much material and arranging it in this easy-to-read fashion is truly stunning.

I'm certain Carl Jung would be thrilled that his many inexplicable adventures are coming together at last, to be studied and appreciated not only by mainstream psychologists and philosophers, but also by students of the unseen worlds of the psychic and paranormal.

It's also interesting to note that Dr. Jung was a believer in God, at a time when the concept of God was being eliminated from the field of science.

As Doug quotes Jung as saying, "We have forgotten the age-old fact that God speaks chiefly through dreams and visions."

So honor your visions. Pay attention to your dreams. Become aware of the synchronicities in your world. You don't know how they will affect your life or the lives of others. Enjoy this collection of amazing experiences. And, I can't help but be curious as to what coincidences and synchronicities await us!

Thanks, Doug, for shining your light on these strange and fascinating events.

Diane L. Ross, Author, hypnotist, speaker Orlando, Florida
September 2014
http://www.dianeross.com

Note from Doug Dillon:

When Diane emailed me the wonderful foreword to this book, she also added a PS. It seemed so pertinent to the topic of purposeful coincidences and Carl Jung's definition of synchronicity that I had to include it. Diane and I occasionally do presentations together and I am honored to have her observations as the lead text for this effort. Here is her P.S., just as she sent them to me.

P.S. to Doug:

Another coincidence: I had recently attended an Internet marketing convention with my husband, Randy. I went just to see musician Vanilla Ice, who was performing as part of the weekend's entertainment. Internet marketing (or any type of marketing) is not my forte. However, a speaker caught my attention when he explained that his next book was simply a compilation of his blog posts.

That information resonated with me. I could blog about the incredible experiences I've had with my clients, and then combine them all in a book.

We had been back from the marketing convention less than a week when Doug called and asked me to write the foreword for his book, which was a compilation of his blogs!

Thank you, universe!

Thank you, God!

Time to start seriously blogging!

Introduction

This book is a direct result of a series of articles I posted on my blog about the great Swiss psychiatrist, Carl Jung. So many people consistently read those postings that it became apparent to me that there are a lot of folks in the world who are as interested in the man and his work as I am. Well, almost.

As a writer of both fiction and nonfiction about things paranormal, my research has often led me to the writings of Dr. Jung. Having been interested in the nature of *coincidences* for many years, I found Jung's idea of synchronicity especially fascinating. In that light, I began to probe into the man's life and writings. But in doing so, I also discovered how Jung had experienced many paranormal events in his life. A few I had run into before, but most were new to me. I put the word *coincidences* in italics here to stress the point of relatedness between events instead of seeing them as just random happenings.

And in reading Jung's own words about those unusual events he experienced, I realized that many of them were probably little known because they were mixed with all of the man's in-depth explanations of things psychological. Such density of material, although it contains valuable information, can be quite hard to plow through for the average reader.

What if, I wondered, I could just tease the bare essence of those stories out of Jung's work and share them with people online through my blog? Add in some pictures to keep the reader's interest and ... Well, that's exactly what I did. The final results were reasonably short postings, bite sized and to the point. Most ran in the 400-600 word count range, but a few approached 1,000.

What began to happen though, as I studied Jung and wrote about him, especially with regard to synchronicity, the meaningful connection between one or more simultaneous events, I began to have some very unique and complex series of *coincidences* occur in my own life. It was as if these events were outer manifestations of my own inner processes. This didn't really startle me because years ago, when my wife Barbara and I wrote our nonfiction book on the paranormal, *An Explosion of Being*, we found the more we concentrated on strange events, the more they happened.

Those intricate coincidences that occurred while working on the Jung postings were truly amazing. So much so, that I posted articles about them on my blog, a series of eleven. And when I did that, even more *synchronistic* events popped up relating to the initial ones. Quite fascinating.

Of course, as a writer about such weird and unusual things, I'm always posting pieces about ghosts, hauntings, mediums, psychics, ESP, etc. Most of them relatively short, illustrated by photos and supported by useful links. And I invite a lot of guest bloggers to add their own stories as well. All of those topics are the type of things that Carl Jung experienced and wrote about in addition to his work on synchronicity.

Up until August of 2014, I had toyed with the idea of actually writing a book that related to Jung somehow, but nothing crystalized in my mind until I checked my blog statistics one evening. What I found was an astounding two-day leap in the number of views on my website – 700%. 700%!

When I looked into it, I found that someone had posted the Carl Jung series links on a well-known online sharing site. What a *coincidence*!

So there you have the trigger that got me going to finally put this book together.

What I did here with this effort was to create the seven separate sections that you will see in the Table of Contents in order to organize all of the Jung postings in a sensible way based upon his experiences. The titles for the Jung material are entirely my own, simplified versions of very long strings of information.

Each section begins with a Jung post and occasionally some of them end with one as well. In addition to the Jung material, I included those other paranormal postings from my blog that support the Jung information in one way or the other. Those articles are either things I have experienced myself or they have come from family, friends or close associates. I wanted to keep the book in that intimate circle of people I know and trust. That was my BS filter working at its best.

The result then is a relatively small book because there are simply fewer extraneous words than usual, the very nature of good blog postings. I also deleted all the photos that went with those articles because they take up too much space, in addition to being a more complex and expensive way to publish.

However, if you would like to see any of those posts in their original forms, just go to the home page of my website and find the last window on the sidebar to the right. That's one of the multiple openings to my blog archive. All you have to do is enter a key word from one of the stories you're interested in and you will find yourself linked to appropriate articles. There is a link to my website at the end of this introduction and at the end of the book.

Within these pages, you will find a great many stories centered in St. Augustine, Florida. Why? For a start, the city is the oldest and most haunted in the United States, and it is my favorite place to visit. Since I live only 100 miles from there, I go quite often. Much of my time in that old city is spent doing research for my young adult paranormal/historical fiction series titled, **The St. Augustine Trilogy**. Furthermore, many of my associates who contributed to this book sent me their own fascinating tales about St. Augustine.

So there you have it. Hope you enjoy what you are about to read. May you find that it adds at least a little to your understanding of the incredible unseen worlds within which we somehow navigate every day of our lives.

Doug Dillon
Altamonte Springs, FL
www.dougdillon.com

Some Initial Food for Thought

1. "As far as we can discern, the sole purpose of human existence is to kindle a light of meaning in the darkness of mere being." ~**Carl Jung**~

2. "Do you imagine the universe is agitated? Go into the desert at night and look at the stars. This practice should answer the question." ~**Lao Tzu**~

3. "There are no mistakes, no coincidences. All events are blessings given to us to learn from." ~**Elizabeth Kubler-Ross**~

4. "The soul of man is immortal and imperishable." ~**Plato**~

5. "Deep in the human unconscious is a pervasive need for a logical universe that makes sense. But the real universe is always one step beyond logic." ~**Frank Herbert, Dune**~

6. "We are just an advanced breed of monkeys on a minor planet of a very average star. But we can understand the Universe. That makes us something very special." ~**Stephen Hawking**~

7. "We are what we think. All that we are arises with our thoughts. With our thoughts, we make the world." ~**Buddha**~

8. "The Universe has shouted itself alive. We are one of the shouts." ~**Ray Bradbury**~

9. "Coincidence is God's way of remaining anonymous." ~**Albert Einstein**~

10. "We have forgotten the age-old fact that God speaks chiefly through dreams and visions." ~**Carl Jung**~

Contents

Section 5

Section 6

Section 7

Section 1

Physical Phenomena

1
Jung: THE SPLIT TABLE

One day during his teenage years, Carl Jung was studying in his room. His door led to the dining room where his mother sat knitting. It was partly closed at the time.

Suddenly the sound of a large bang, like a gunshot, shattered the silence. It had come from the dining room. Jung jumped up and ran to see what had made the noise. There he found his mother looking very startled, her knitting having fallen to the floor. "What happened?" She asked, then telling her son the sound had come from somewhere very near to her.

As Jung and his mother searched the room for the source of the noise, their eyes came to rest on the dining room table. It had split wide open. Astounded, Jung inspected the table and found that the fracture had occurred within the solid oak itself and not along any connecting joints.

This discovery led to quite a commotion in the family, obviously because no one could figure out how such a thing might happen. Having belonged to Jung's grandmother when she was young, the table was anything but new. Green wood might split but certainly not oak that had aged so long. Besides, there were no fluctuations in the weather conditions that might cause such a thing. No one ever came up with a plausible explanation for the event.

Soon after the incident with the table, something else startling happened, again in the dining room (See Chapter 8 tilted Jung: THE KNIFE). These two events, when taken together, seem to be primary among the many in his youth that would propel Jung into investigations of the paranormal.

2
A Car Horn and an Appearance

Paranormal occurrences that affect physical things or impact people in other ways? This story tells about two such events and they come directly from my own history. In fact, they were the sparks that put my wife Barbara and myself on a road to intense paranormal exploration. I wrote about those experiences in the book I co-authored with Barb titled, *An Explosion of Being: An American Family's Journey into the Psychic*. So, instead of rewriting that material, I copied it directly from the book and reproduced it here.

You see, this all happened shortly after my dad died. I was in my early 30s and shattered by the loss of my father. As part of trying to help my mother settle Dad's affairs, we were at her house when the first event occurred. Since Dad was a retired military officer, the Air Force had sent representatives to assist Mom in acquiring her benefits. We'll pick up the story as those people arrive at the house:

"During one of those hectic days soon after Dad's death, a shiny blue Air Force car pulled into the driveway of my parents' home. Two very somber sergeants, well-practiced in the ways of grief and the details of military benefits, stepped out of the shimmering August heat into the coolness of the air conditioned house.

"Sid Brewer, a family friend and retired Air Force officer, was there to guide us through the detailed procedures. Sid and I sat facing the two sergeants over the dining room table, by then covered with documents. The exchange of necessary information droned on for a while, until my attention was diverted.

"'Whoever is blowing that damned car horn had better cut it out,' I thought angrily. The noise continued, until I finally got up and opened the front door. Now the sound blasted through the heat, further stirring my anger. No strange cars were visible, just the Air Force vehicle and Dad's empty car parked under the oak tree a short distance away.

"The blowing horn was coming from Dad's car! Sid and I opened the hood and pulled out the wires, resulting in exquisite silence. 'Must have been the heat that set it off,' Sid commented. I agreed, but somehow the event jarred my already unsettled psyche.

"The next morning presented a raft of estate-settling tasks. My plans included using Dad's Ford to make my rounds of the Social Security and V.A. offices, but I hated to drive without a horn. Just on the chance that the problem had rectified itself, I reattached the wires. No exploding repetition of yesterday's noise, so with a couple of test honks, off I went to downtown Orlando and my list of appointments.

"The Social Security office was overflowing with people. When my turn finally came, the representative was helpful and efficient. Briefcase in hand, I was soon out the door, walking toward the parking lot. Dad's car was angle-parked only a short distance from me, and in a few steps, I was directly in front of it. My mind was a jumble of sadness and financial details, when suddenly the car horn went off with another continuing blast that shook every fiber in my body.

"I was stunned. For an instant, I froze in mid-stride and automatically looked for a driver sitting in the front seat. No, no one was there—just me and this crazy car blowing its brains out. Once the wires were disconnected again, I continued my errands but with an uneasiness that could not readily be put aside.

"After those two events, Barb, Mom and I wondered if just maybe Dad was trying to communicate with us. In the end, I rejected that possibility until I told my aunt and uncle about the car horn events during a phone conversation. Only then did they tell us they had actually seen dad in their living room on the day of his death. They didn't want to tell us because they didn't think we would have believed them. They lived 1,200 away."

3
The Owl and the Trashcan

Ever have things move in your house without anybody actually touching them? Try this story on for size.

One day my wife Barbara and I were sitting in our family room talking to our son, Greg. During that conversation, we heard something hit the floor in the foyer that was on the other side of a wall. Whatever it was even bounced a few times.

We looked at each other as if we expected answers, but when none came, Greg got up to check. As he disappeared into the foyer, we heard him say, "Whoa! How could that happen?" He then reappeared with an owl made of painted tree bark that usually sits in a tall artificial tree near the front door.

"That's what made the noise?" I asked.

"Um-hm," Greg replied. "Somehow it came out of the tree and ended up at the other side of the foyer. Even if it did pop loose from the tree by itself, there's no way it could bounce all that distance (about 8 feet). It looks like it had to have been thrown."

That's when I remembered the crystal owl my dad had given my mom many years before, which also sat in a display case in our foyer. In fact, my mom had a collection of owls. Sharing my immediate reaction with Barb and Greg that this event might have been caused by my deceased mother, I still wondered if there was any way that the tree bark owl could have reasonably bounced its way across eight feet of hard flooring caused by normal physical forces.

The next day, I decided to test this possibility. To do so, I simply dropped the owl a number of times from its normal perch in the foyer tree to see what would happen. It did bounce, but less than half the distance it had traveled the day before. Greg was right. There was no way that owl could have covered the distance it did the day before without some help.

That got me to thinking because a way I test whether or not an event is paranormal is to see if one or more other recent happenings seemed unusual as well. I've found that the linkage between such situations is what helps to verify their paranormal nature.

In this case, a few days before the owl fell, something happened in our garage that startled me. While working in there, I started to walk past a trashcan when the lid suddenly shut with a forceful noise. I realized I must not have closed the thing fully, but it looked and sounded just as it usually did when I used my hand to push it down. Besides, for such a thing to happen exactly as I approached the trashcan was just a little too *coincidental*.

Just as with the owl, I tested the lid by seeing if I could get it to close by itself and with as much force. It took some work to balance it properly, but I could only get the lid to shut on its own if I tapped on the can or nudged it. Even then, the force of that closing didn't come close to what I experienced initially.

Final conclusion? Two tested events occurring within a few days of each other, and happening just at the right time, spells unusual causation and purpose of some kind, at least to my way of thinking. Did they occur because my mom was trying to say hello or did they happen for some other reason? Who knows?

I've gotten to the point over the years that I try not to make that final determination. There are simply too many possibilities to say for sure. What I do know is that, for me, such circumstances are like little comforting flashes of light in the darkness that simply say, "Pay attention and remember this. You are connected to All That Is in wondrous ways."

4
A Horse at the Door

Here is a tale my grandmother told me when I was a kid relating to her own childhood:

The home where she grew up in New York City sat at the bottom of a slight hill. The house was actually at a crossroads. She could look out her front door and stare directly up a street that ended at the road where she lived. And in those days, even in New York, there were still a lot of horse-drawn wagons.

Occasionally, she said, the family could hear a horse coming fast down that street opposite her house. It never slowed down, got louder and louder as it approached, and then slammed into their front door with a terrible crash. Time after time, family members rushed to open the door only to find nothing—no horse and no marks on the door.

When I asked her what she thought about those experiences, she said she figured that long before her family moved in, a horse had actually smacked into their house, and what they heard were just echoes of the past.

I often ask myself how I would react if I continually had something like that happen. What about you?

5
A Noise in the Cellar

This is the first of four stories shared with me by my French friend and fellow author, Patrick Delsaut:

In the early 1990s, a strange phenomenon occurred in the cellar of my home.

It was night and all was quiet. Suddenly my sister opened the cellar door for some reason and from its depths gushed a strange sound vaguely resembling a whirring electric motor. This amazed and frightened her because we kept no engines, boilers, motorbikes or any other kind of equipment down there that could produce such a sound.

I came running immediately when my sister called me to hear this weird, whirring noise. Sure enough, our usually silent cellar had somehow been invaded by a sound that shouldn't be there. How surprising! In fact, I had never heard anything exactly like that before.

After some hesitation, I decided to go and investigate. With each step though, the noise increased in intensity and surrounded me. Once I got all the way down, I looked around but could not find the source of all that racket.

I then asked my sister to come down so that she could also observe this phenomenon firsthand. After she joined me, we thoroughly inspected every corner of the cellar with our eyes, our ears and our hands. The pipes, walls and floor didn't vibrate, nor did the gas and water meters. We could find nothing that might explain this loud and unpleasant noise.

We wondered if the sound could be coming from one of our neighbors on either side of us, but we finally discovered its intensity increased slightly near the basement windows (vents) overlooking the street.

Thinking something may be going on outside our home, we charged up the stairs and out onto the street. Nothing. All was silent. As soon as we went back into the house and opened the cellar door, however, the same vibrating noise assaulted us again. It evidently had not stopped in our absence whatever its origins.

The next day, the sound was gone, but as soon as night fell, the strange vibration came back! My sister and I continued our investigations, but we discovered nothing new. It went on like that for several nights in succession, and then stopped for a while before resuming once again. A short time later though, the sound disappeared forever.

To this day, I have no explanation for what my sister and I experienced.

6
Banging in the Cupboard

Story Number two out of four from my French friend and fellow author Patrick Delsaut:

In 1991, I was awakened several times one morning by a rapid, repetitive knocking coming from a cupboard located at the foot of my bed. It sounded like someone banging with a small hard object on wood but with a particular resonance. Very unusual. This happened on many days, always in the morning, but they stopped when I awakened.

At that time, the houses on either side of mine were totally unoccupied, so the sounds couldn't have come from the neighbors. However, the history of those people, especially the ones who used to live on the other side of the cupboard, made me wonder.

You see, it had recently been the home of an elderly, mentally ill gentleman who died there, violently. At one time, he lived there with his elderly mother. The police found him dead, sitting on a chair in the middle of a room whose walls were sprayed with blood as if his arteries had exploded. Very strange indeed. Restoration plans for this man's house had been made, but work had not yet begun. The place was still empty when I started hearing noises in my cupboard.

The other former neighbor, who was about the same age as the first, had also died recently. He also lived alone, but his elderly, mentally ill mother had stayed with him until her death. Here you see a contrast with the first neighbor I mentioned.

Mental illness plagued both households, the son in one and the mother in the other.

These two neighbors, whose destinies are strangely close with regard to time of death and the aspect of mental illness, might suggest that there is a relationship of cause and effect. In short, let's not mince words, it sounds like a ghost story! Ghosts who would have given repeated blows in my cupboard! Even so, something in me said that's not what it was. In fact, it seemed to be more like a Poltergeist (" knocking spirit" in German) than a ghost.

Of course, I tried to reproduce these sounds using my hand, nails, a pencil, a pen, a screwdriver, etc., without success. None of those matched what I heard. These had a subtle resonance quite particular, both clear and deep, close and distant, impossible to reproduce.

Like other similar things that have happened to me, I have no final explanation as to the cause of this knocking.

7
Molly's Doll

AGhost hunting story from my friends Mary Jo Fister and Greg Bush from Offthetrails Paranormal investigations:

In June 2012, Off the Trails Paranormal Investigations revisited Miss Caroline's Guest House in St. Augustine, Florida. This is a lovely Victorian house that has been a veterinarian office, a TB hospital, and a private home. We had been there once before and had some activity. Unfortunately, the Guest House has now been turned into a restaurant.

This time, we set up for three days, and were rewarded with some great video evidence!

We set up our static night vision cameras, did baseline readings with the meters, and made our headquarters the Colonel's Room.

There are three haunted guest rooms, known as the Colonel's Room, Miss Margaret's, or Molly's Room, and Rose's room. There are several spirits who inhabit the house, according to owner Tina Danielson, including Ulysses, Charlie, Miss Lucy (aka Rose), Colonel Kennedy, and little Molly.

Colonel Kennedy was the father of Ulysses and Molly. The Colonel, a Union officer, and Molly, are the most active.

Molly is believed to be five-years old. In her room there are some toys to encourage the child to interact with guests. We played with Molly using a doll that is motion sensitive, plays peek-a-boo and talks.

We realized in the morning the doll was on the floor, but didn't know how that happened. I picked it up, sat it securely on the horse's back, and went to make coffee. When I came back in, the doll was again on the floor. Once more, I put the doll firmly in the saddle.

As Greg and I watched, the doll flew off the horse again! We were amazed and excited to see it! It was later, reviewing the film from our static night vision camera that we caught the spirit of Molly playing with her doll. In addition, the REM Pod went off several times, as evidence that Molly, or some spirit, was there.

We also have photographic evidence in the upstairs sitting room of an energy ball, and spikes on the Mel Meter (a device that measures temperature and electromagnetic fields). Rob heard footsteps around 3: 30 AM, when we were the only ones in the house, and he was the only one awake.

Many people have experienced paranormal activity here, from hearing footsteps, to being touched, to smelling roses. Tina Danielson and Miss Caroline's are featured on a "My Ghost Story" segment.

8
Jung: THE KNIFE

Two weeks after a solid oak table had inexplicably split near where he was studying in his room during his teenage years, Jung came home to find everyone in his house visibly upset. His mother, sister and the maid all had the same story.

An hour before his arrival, there had been another loud explosion in the dining room just like the one he and his mother experienced when their table split. The family thought it might have come from that same table, but they could find no new splits in the wood. After looking the table over himself, Jung agreed that it contained no new cracks.

Another piece of furniture in the room was a large, wooden buffet or sideboard, where the family kept silverware and other dining items. He thought maybe that wood had split, but after inspecting it, he could find no cracks in it either.

Then on a hunch, he decided to look in a cupboard of the sideboard. There he found a basket of bread that also contained the shattered remains of a heavy steel bread knife. Jung located those pieces of metal in different corners of the basket. According to the family, the knife had been used just a short time before the explosion.

Wanting to investigate further, Jung took the metal pieces to a knife maker. When the man examined them with a magnifying glass, he said they looked as if the blade had exploded. He told Jung he could find no flaws in the metal and went on to say it would have taken a tremendous forced effort to produce such an effect.

Section 2

Haunted Places

9
Jung: THE HAUNTED COTTAGE

In the summer of 1920, Carl Jung was invited to give a long series of lectures in London. To give these talks though, he had to find a place to stay. A friend finally located a lovely little cottage for an unusually cheap price and rented it for him.

During the time Jung lived at the cottage, the friend who found it for him occasionally visited overnight, as did others. Evidently, everyone enjoyed being there but Jung.

At the end of his first week of giving lectures, Jung went to bed around 11:00 PM. Tired but not actually very sleepy, he just lay there in bed. Seconds later, he found he wasn't able to move. Not only that, the room seemed stuffy and some sort of bad smell filled the air.

Finally willing himself to get up, he lit a candle. Immediately the smell went away, but he only slept after dawn broke.

That next night, the same things happened as before, while other people were staying with him; stuffiness in the room, hard for him to move and the bad smell. Added to all those experiences, however, was a constant dripping sound—one drip every two seconds, according to Jung. He thought the roof must be leaking.

Again, willing himself to get out of bed, he lit a candle and searched for the leak. The dripping sound continued as he looked around.

The ceiling showed nothing, so he followed the sound of the drips. When he located the exact spot where the noise came from on the floor, the sound stopped. The thing is, there was no water anywhere. That next morning he asked his guests if they slept well and they all said they had.

Unhappily for Jung, all the above phenomena happened the following night with more added. This time there were loud noises, like rustling, creaking and knocking. He also had the distinct sensation that a dog was running around his room. The poor man was only able to sleep at dawn when all the commotion came to a complete stop. Apparently, no one else in the house heard, smelled or felt any of this.

Very frustrated, Jung eventually spoke to one of the maids. He noticed that after serving dinner in the evening, they scurried out of the cottage very quickly and went home.

When he asked them about their behavior, they said the place was haunted and they didn't want to be there after dark. Evidently, everyone in the neighborhood knew this. That's why the rent was so cheap, they told him.

Armed with this information, Jung shared it with the friend who rented the house for him. The friend only laughed.

Poor Jung. All of the phenomena continued and one night he turned over in bed to find himself looking at the partial face of an old woman lying next to him. That did it. He leaped out of bed and spent the rest of the night in a chair. After that, he moved to another room where he wasn't bothered at all.

When he told his friend about moving, the friend laughed at him again. That caused Jung to challenge this man to stay in his, Jung's, room overnight when no one else would be in the cottage. His friend agreed, but decided that if there were ghosts, they could be anywhere in the house. So instead of sleeping where Jung had, he stayed in the cottage's main room. Interestingly enough, he brought a shotgun with him.

The friend set himself up as if camping and just as he was falling asleep, he heard something. It sounded like footsteps in a nearby hallway. Taking a candle with him, he looked but saw nothing.

That made him so uncomfortable that he closed the door leading to that hallway. But there was no key. Since he couldn't lock the door, he shoved a chair up against it. That gives you a good look at the man's state of mind. No doubt he kept his shotgun nearby. How he intended to use it on ghosts is unclear.

Just as he settled back down for the night, Jung's friend once again heard footsteps in the hallway. This time they stopped just on the other side of the door. Seconds later, the chair he had put up against that door creaked as if someone were pushing it.

Immediately, he jumped up, grabbed his camping equipment and spent the rest of the night in the garden where he slept undisturbed. Later when he spoke to Jung, Jung told him he would never stay another night in the cottage.

10
Poltergeists

I'm willing to bet that if most people talked with members of their families, they would come up with stories of all sorts of paranormal activity. I'm not just talking about immediate families, I'm talking about grandparents, aunts, uncles and cousins.

In my case, my mom's relatives were the ones who told such tales. For me, I found those stories so interesting because they came from people who never usually expressed an interest or even belief in such things.

Mom's family all came from the New York City, Connecticut region. One summer when I was a teenager, we had a big family gathering and I got a chance to speak with one of her cousins and her husband. Both were involved with real estate and told a story about visiting a particular house they were trying to sell for some clients. It was nighttime and the owners were away.

The place was dark and they approached using flashlights. But just as they got to the front door, noises exploded from inside the house. Frightened and thinking vandals must be inside, they rushed back towards their car. They told me it sounded like a group of people was destroying everything they could find. As quickly as it started though, all those noises stopped.

After waiting a few minutes, they crept back up to house. No more sounds, and in fact, looking through the windows with their flashlights, they couldn't see any damage. Thinking that rather odd, they decided to go in and look around. Pretty brave if you ask me, but they did it. Once inside, they found no damage whatsoever and nothing out of place. That frightened them even more than the sounds themselves and they had no explanation for what happened. Now, we would probably identify such an experience as poltergeists.

So, the next time you have any kind of family gathering or reunion, ask people about their strange experiences. You might be very surprised with who comes up with some very weird but interesting tales.

11
The Spark in the Road

A very different kind of ghost story:

I find that paranormal experiences aren't always recognized as such at the time. For me, odd or strange events only get defined as paranormal after further thought and investigation. This happened a number of years ago when I saw something in the road on my way to work.

Way back then, I was teaching at Ocoee Middle School in the western part of Orange County, Florida. To get there, I had to take a country road. Beautiful drive in the early morning, so much nicer than fighting I-4 traffic going into and out of Orlando on a daily basis.

On this particular day, about half way to school, the road ahead stretched out into the surrounding light mist, but wasn't obstructed by it. Quite a distance ahead, something flickered, ever so slightly. It seemed to be a small flashing of light on the road itself.

At first, I thought I was imagining it because the thing was so small.

I blinked my eyes a couple of times, but whatever it was didn't go away. In fact, it got larger and more distinct the further I drove.

Then at about 100 feet away, it looked like a shimmering, flickering spark about a foot or two high and maybe six to eight inches wide.

Astounded, I lifted my foot off the accelerator. As soon as I did, the spark vanished. In it's place, I could see a dead animal. When I got there, I realized that it was a large raccoon. No sign of the spark.

Weird, right? But I didn't have time to dally and figure it out. School awaited, so off I went.

That evening though, I shared my experience with my wife Barbara. Intrigued, she offered to do some channeling and see if we could get an explanation. Our book on the paranormal, *An Explosion of Being,* had just been published and Barb was still channeling from what we had come to call, The Source.

In this instance, The Source said the raccoon had been so freshly killed that its spirit had not yet adjusted to its death. The essence of the creature was simply hanging around the body trying to figure out what happened. I had read stories about humans having such experiences, but it never occurred to me animals might have similar experiences.

12
The King and the Prince

For our anniversary in 2009, my wife Barb and I treated ourselves by spending a few days on St. Simon's Island, Georgia. Beautiful place with a long history that connects with St. Augustine in our home state of Florida.

In our travels on that island, we visited what's left of Fort Frederica, a crucial British outpost just before the Revolutionary War. The fort itself is very small, but the surrounding area is huge because an entire town once existed there as well. When the British abandoned the fort though, the town died. All that you can see of it today are the foundations of houses and businesses.

Our home base for all of our excursions was the gorgeous King and Prince Resort. It's a very comfortable place right on the ocean and dates back to 1935.

Maybe it was our day of exploring that eerie Fort Frederica ghost town without anyone else around, but something happened at the King and Prince to make us wonder. After dinner that evening, we decided to check out the hotel's solarium, a sort of sun room area used for events like small banquets.

It was just Barb and me. That whole area of the hotel seemed as abandoned as the town near Fort Frederica, totally quiet except for our conversation.

We spent some time looking at the furnishings and decor before finally plopping ourselves down in two Wingback chairs.

After a while, we both fell silent, lost in our own thoughts. It's at that point I had a distinct sensation Barb and I weren't alone. I kept looking around to make sense out of what I was feeling, but couldn't. Seconds later, Barb broke the silence and told me she was having similar thoughts.

Realizing we were both on the same track, we decided to just sit silently for a while and tune in to whatever seemed to be happening near or around us. This we did for about five minutes and then shared whatever sensations, thoughts or feelings bubbled up in the quiet.

The result was fascinating. I would say a few words, then Barb, and then me again—back and forth as if we were both describing the exact same scene. When we got done speaking, we just looked at each other in wonder.

What we had jointly described were the sights and sounds of a party going on in the solarium. It was as if people were walking around—people of a bygone era. There was music, laughter, food and drink being served and some people were playing games. Glasses, dishes and utensils clinked. Amazing. It gave us chills.

No, we didn't actually see or hear those things. It was more like we were mentally tuning into a television program, a reality show in which we were somehow distant participants.

Our conclusion? We as human beings are connected to All That Is, has been and will be. Sometimes, especially in the stillness and quiet of the moment, we are privileged to perceive some of those connections. That night we were simply thankful to have received such a gift. A further explanation simply wasn't needed.

13
Ghost Hunting in a Bookstore

Awhile back, it was my pleasure to be a co-presenter with Mary Jo Fister and Greg Bush from Offthetrails Paranormal Investigations (OPI) at the Orlando Public Library. That evening I then joined them for a ghost hunt at Paula Thompsons' Here Be Dragons Bookshoppe in Winter Garden, Florida. What a great adventure with lots of activity. Sadly though, that book store went out of business about a year later.

Below you will find the OPI posting about that event. And below that you see some of my comments about my own experiences at the time:

"When our friend Doug Dillon suggested Here Be Dragons as an investigation site, he told us the owner had been experiencing activity. Nobody was being hurt, but she would find books stacked on the floor when she opened in the morning, and they weren't there when she closed in the evening! Books would sometimes fly off the shelves! We love books and reading, so the idea of spending time in the store really appealed to us!

"Paula, the owner, told us the activity had quieted some in recent months. Her daughter had refused to stay in the shop alone. The store had been a thrift shop and children's clothing store before Paula took over the space. Originally, it was a Western Union place, and the sliding metal door and barred window in the back of the store are the reminders.

"Angel and I did our baseline sweeps. We found nothing unusual. There were spikes near the fuse box, but we expected that! Doug's books are carried there, and we checked those for residual energy, but found nothing. We set up our static night vision cameras with the monitors. We left the Mel Meters set up to catch any activity: one in the front and one in the back.

"While Greg and Doug snapped photos, Angel and Rob watched the monitors, and I set up EVP (electronic voice phenomenon) sessions. I employed the camera, Ovilus, or ghost box (a radio receiver that is supposed to pick up spirit transmissions and put them into words), and flashlight! That flashlight is one of our favorite tools! Its magic was with us tonight! I started in the back of the store. The flashlight did nothing. The words "fact, word, and verbs" came through the Ovilus. They seemed relevant to the space.

"Next, I started a spirit box session. It was very fruitful! A girl's voice said 'Pamela'. In answer to my question about throwing the books, we heard 'No' and 'No one' in a male voice. 'I did 'em' was the answer to my query about standing the books on the floor. Another voice said "hip hop" for no apparent reason. When I asked, 'What color is my shirt?' responses were white, grey, and purple. In reality, my shirt was black. Remember that ghosts may not see in our spectrum! When I was ending the session, I asked if there was anything else anyone wanted to say. 'Don't give up!' and 'F — you!' were my answers.

"I moved to the tiny alcove. The Ovilus relayed the words 'Lynn, focus, cloister, and Japanese' which seemed relevant, especially cloister. Japanese, however, had us baffled.

"My final spot was near the front of the store. This is where we had our best results! The Ovilus relayed a laugh for some reason. Then the spirit box said 'Can you say f — it?' The Ovilus then gave us the word 'laugh.' Clearly, there was a joker with us. Suddenly, a pile of books behind me fell over. I had not bumped them!

"Paula laughed and said the place where I was sitting is the spot she had the paranormal books until just the other day! The flashlight was on, and I asked, 'If someone is here and wants to turn this off, go ahead.' The flashlight went off, and the conversation began! (This type of communication happens when the flashlight goes on and off by itself in response to questions.)

"The ghost told us he is a Cuban boy, between the ages of 10 and 15. His name is Eric. He lived before 1950, and came to the US with friends. He told us he is in the shop alone. However, he may have been mistaken, or misleading us.

"Other voices came to us on the spirit box! However, Eric did admit to us, after a little prodding that it was he who stacked and threw the books. He came to Here Be Dragons in a case of books as an attachment haunting! He said he wanted people to know he was there. He confessed that he was lonely, and never left the shop.

"Paula agreed to say 'hello' and 'good bye' each day. She also told Eric she would tell some of her customers about him, and ask them to talk to him, too. Eric spoke to us for a very long time, much longer than most other ghosts! He told us he liked classical music, and Paula said she'd play that more often.

"The group of us spoke about books, and when Lemony Snicket came up, the Ovilus said 'twist.' During the flashlight session, the Ovilus said very little.

"When I asked, in a spirit box session, if he could see Doug, a voice through the spirit box replied, 'I see 'im.' In answer to the question about my hair color, (blonde) voices said 'purple and aqua!' When I asked, 'How many of us are here?' The response was, '4 women and 3 men.' Who weren't they counting?

"We did several flashlight sessions with Eric. During one of those, there is unexplained music and a little girl said, 'Mommy!' Might it be his little sister?

"We still have questions about the store. Who might be the other voices? We wish Eric all the best, and hope he and

Paula and the store's customers continue to peacefully co-exist. We are glad Doug was able to be there! We will stop by the next time we are in the area!

Observations from My Point of View that Night (From the author, Doug Dillon)

At one point in the investigation, I walked over to where the monitors were located for keeping track of any activity captured on the two TV cameras that had been set up. As I watched the monitor on the left, a pinpoint of light spiraled from deep in the store right up to the camera that was just behind me.

It then spiraled backward the way it came. That all happened within a couple of seconds or even less.

While Mary Jo talked to the spirit named Eric, I sat on the floor about six feet behind her. All of a sudden, another pinpoint of light popped on and then off in my peripheral vision—to my right. It appeared in a bookcase, below the shelf where OPI has stationed one of their pieces of energy sensing equipment. Mary Jo and Greg studied that video at a later time and were never able to figure out what had been recorded.

14
Castillo Footprints in Time

As a Florida writer of fiction and nonfiction, I get to explore some of my favorite topics that include both the paranormal and Florida history. And that includes the oldest and most haunted city in the U.S., St. Augustine.

Ghost stories abound in that town as do ghost tours of all kinds. Paranormal investigators make regular stops there and probe every nook and cranny.

One of the most visited places in the city is the old stone fort, the Castillo de San Marcos. Completed by the Spanish in 1695, that site literally swims in legends and myth. Much has been written about the Castillo, both historically and in the paranormal realm, but I won't bore you with all that old information.

What I want to share with you now, however, are two quick stories that I stumbled over one day when visiting the fort and doing research for the third book in my young adult series titled, **The St. Augustine Trilogy.**

But since both of these tales come from people directly associated with the Castillo, they asked that I not mention their names or positions within the organization. Gotta protect my sources.

On the day of my visit, I found a person who seemed to be in a position of authority. I was interested in certain aspects of the Castillo's construction.

We had a nice chat and in the conversation I told him I write about things paranormal as well as historical. "Oh ho," he replied with a grin, "you need to talk to Alberta (not her name)."

I had no idea who *Alberta* was or why I should talk to her. And just as I started to ask, she, Alberta, walked up to us, pointed to her watch and said to my companion, "It's working again. Can you believe it?"

Turns out that every time Alberta enters the Castillo, her watch stops working. It usually remains inoperable for no reason she can discover until she leaves the building. And on that day, oddly, the watch began ticking away only as she approached me and the other person.

That's when the man I was talking to originally took me aside and said, "If you won't use my name, I'll tell you about a series of identical experiences a close family member had here a number of years ago."

Now that is just the kind of comment I love: from someone who is definitely not looking for notoriety and who is in a position to really know something of value.

After I agreed, he said, "This family member used to work in the gift shop downstairs (on the ground floor of the fort). It was her job to open the doors to the shop every morning. "At times, the air conditioning would create a slick film of condensation on the stone floor, revealing small footprints; barefoot, like those of a child.

"Of course, there was no way that could happen because the shop is locked up all night and stays locked until the next morning."

My companion offered no explanation because he didn't have any. But the gravity with which he revealed this little mystery told me he was indeed, telling the truth as he knew it.

The final interesting item here is that the onsite research I was doing that day at the Castillo related to the final book of my young adult, paranormal/historical trilogy, titled *Targeting Orion's Children*. In that book, there is an attacking entity disguised as a ten-year-old child known as Evil Boy. His domain is the Castillo where the book's climax takes place. Ten-year-old boy? Footprints of a child in the Castillo's gift shop? Hmm.

Being too good to pass up, I inserted both those stories told to me in the draft of *Targeting Orion's Children.*

15
Ghost Lighthouse, St. Augustine, Florida

In addition to the Carl Jung series, this posting on my blog gets an extraordinary number of hits on a daily basis:

Since so many paranormal events have occurred at the St. Augustine Lighthouse, I decided to pull together some key information from various sources into this one posting.

Over the years, visitors and staff members alike have definitely experienced a lot of strange things. Many paranormal investigators have studied the lighthouse, including the popular TV team, *Ghost Hunters*. So if you haven't visited the place, put it on your "to do at some point in my lifetime" list.

Historical Background

The present day lighthouse sits at the northern tip of Anastasia Island directly across Matanzas Bay from downtown St. Augustine. In the evening, from downtown, you can see its beam sweep across those waters and then shift out over the Atlantic.

Erected in 1874, the building was preceded by a coquina stone structure originally built by the Spanish. In fact, the Spanish had maintained a watchtower near the present day site ever since their arrival during the late 1500s. Before the Europeans arrived, of course, Native Americans freely roamed the area.

What People Experience at the Lighthouse Itself

- Each night, staff members lock the door at the top of the lighthouse that leads outside to the viewing balcony. Periodically, they find the door open in the morning. There is a security system, but no alarms sound.

- On occasion, people see the figure of a man at the top of the lighthouse at night even though the place is closed and locked.

- At times, people smell cigar smoke at the base of the lighthouse. It is always cigar smoke and there are strict "No Smoking" signs everywhere on the lighthouse grounds.

A Special Lighthouse Story

Even though the lighthouse became automated in 1955, someone still needed to monitor the beacon in case something went wrong. One night, the caretaker realized the light had actually ceased functioning. Immediately, he walked rapidly in the darkness from the old light keeper's house towards the lighthouse entrance.

With each step though, he thought he heard someone walking behind him on the gravel walkway. But when he turned around, there was no one there.

Brushing off his experience as imagination, he continued walking only to once again hear those gravely footsteps behind him. Again, he still found himself alone.

Unnerved a bit at this point, the man rushed into the lighthouse and up the stairs. This time though, he could hear footsteps ringing on the metal stairs behind him.

When he finally got to the top and checked the lighting mechanism, he found nothing wrong. As he threw the switch to restart everything, the beacon began functioning again. Not wasting any time or waiting to listen to phantom footsteps, he ran down the 207 metal steps. For three nights in a row after that event, the beacon again stopped working. Just like before, the caretaker found nothing wrong and was followed just as he had been that first time. He did, however, acquire the habit of taking a flashlight and gun with him whenever he went to the lighthouse after sundown.

The Lighthouse Keeper's House (Serves now as a museum)

- Some sort of presence is often felt.

- People get startled by their experiences, but don't seemed to be threatened by them.

- People often experience cold spots.

- In the brick bottom floor, where the old cistern is located, people have seen the shape of a tall man. One staff member saw this shape in a doorway. It appeared gray in color against the dark room beyond. As the staff member stared in disbelief, the shape simply merged with the darkness.

- At times, chairs are moved or overturned

- In the gift shop, staff and volunteers will find items have been moved out of place overnight. Sometimes items disappear only to reappear at a later date. Music boxes will turn on by themselves.

The Light Keeper's House, Yet Again

In the 1960s, the old Light Keeper's house was rented to a man who periodically had guests. On two different occasions, guests reported seeing the exact same thing: A little girl in a frilly dress who stands in a doorway and then disappears.

Tracing Some of These Paranormal Events to the Past

- One unverified story is that someone, a Light Keeper or a helper, hanged himself from the lighthouse.

Another more traceable story has it that a tragedy happened during the construction of the present day lighthouse. Five little girls were playing in a handcar set on a railroad track. Somehow the handcar went out of control and ended up in water where three of the children drowned. Two of them were the daughters of the construction supervisor for the lighthouse.

16
The Bathroom Ghost?

In the original of this post, I included a photo, yes, of one of the bathrooms in my house. In that photo, you can see a window and a shower curtain. Superimposed over those items is a large, filmy, transparent blob that, to me, looks like a head and shoulders. I'll let my original wording take over and then at the end, I will add two fascinating updates:

The picture in question should have been a simple, unremarkable photo, but somehow it turned into something else. The thing is though, the context within which I took it.

You see, a friend called and asked me to join him at his home last Sunday when visitors were to arrive. Turns out, those visitors where ghost hunters. My friend had invited them in to investigate some paranormal activity and he wanted me to participate.

I agreed and had a great time watching Greg Bush and his wife, Mary Jo Fister do an initial analysis of the situation. While they worked, sometimes in the dark, I took my own photos. That story is for another posting.

Unfortunately, all my pictures showed nothing unusual except for one photo that was a part of a preliminary series I took in my bathroom, just before going over to my friend's house. Why the bathroom, you say? Well, I'm very much an amateur photographer. Knowing I might have to try taking pictures that night in near darkness, I wanted to try doing so ahead of time.

When I took this photo, it was almost dark outside. Just a little light was coming through the window at the top of the picture. None of the other shots I took in the bathroom showed anything like the cloudy swath that appears in that picture. Thinking I might have gotten some reflection from the window or continuation of the light from outside, I later took additional pictures in that same spot but couldn't reproduce the results shown in that one photo.

My son, Greg, a professional photographer, analyzed the photo from a lot of aspects and couldn't figure it out. As in anything that *seems* paranormal, I definitely wanted to find any natural, physical causes, but the result of Greg's analysis only deepened the mystery.

The ghost hunt team I mentioned earlier is called, **Offthetrails Paranormal Investigations.** They have done some great work in many places, including my favorite city of all time, St. Augustine, Florida. When I sent them the photo, they were unable to debunk it or explain it in any way.

Update # 1: About a year or so after that event, I was sitting on my sofa in our family room, facing the short hallway leading to the bathroom mentioned above. My wife Barbara was there and I was speaking to her when I happened to glance in the direction of the hallway. What I saw was a dark, yet transparent shadow in the general shape of a head. It was perhaps five to six feet off the ground and as soon as I noticed it, the thing moved rapidly back into the darkened hallway. My impression, for whatever reason, was that this *object/head* realized it was being observed and didn't want that to continue.

I stopped my conversation with Barb and told her what I had just seen. And in our discussion, I mentioned the "bathroom ghost" photo and wondered aloud if there was any connection. Of course, at that time, there wasn't enough information to actually reach any conclusion, so I just mentally filed all that away for future reference.

Update # 2: In the structuring of this book, I originally had no intention of including what you have already read in this story. In my estimation, there was simply not enough information to point to anything conclusive. Well, just maybe there is now, so here we go.

Again, as often happens in the paranormal, and in the world of synchronous events, things tend to occur when you are focused on them. This past weekend, two weeks after putting all the other chapters for this book together, Barb and I had some more experiences.

Our son, Greg, asked us to take care of his new dog for a day while he went on a photo shoot. He's a professional photographer and didn't want to leave his cute little puppy, Chloe, all alone at his house. Being the dog lovers that we are, Barb and I readily agreed. We had great fun with Miss Chloe and when I had to do some writing on the computer in my office, she would wander in and stay with me for a while, sleeping on the floor. My office is right next to the bathroom and hallway already discussed.

At some point in the evening, Chloe walked out of my office and immediately began barking. It was what I call an "intruder" bark in dogs, not vicious, but very defensive and protective. Obviously, she had adopted Barb and me into her pack. And when I looked behind me, Chloe was standing in front of the bathroom and looking down that short hallway as she continued to bark rapidly and loudly, with no tail wagging at all.

I jumped out of my seat and when I got to Chloe, I saw Barb facing the two of us as she stood far back at the end of the family room. She had come in from the kitchen to see what all the fuss was about. In the space between Chloe and Barb, there was nothing to be seen, but Chloe went on with her fussing, *as if* she could see something. It was only when Barb and I spoke to her gently and petted her, did she calm down, stop barking and begin to wag her tail again.

For about thirty minutes after all that commotion, Chloe slept peacefully back in my office near my chair until I got up once again, this time to look for Barb and ask her a question. With Chloe at my heels, I found her in the kitchen. Immediately, Chloe turned around, faced the family room, and began to bark that same intense "intruder alert."

Exactly as she started barking though, all of the lights in the house dimmed, and I don't mean just a quick reduction. No, it was a gradual dimming that held for a few seconds before full power resumed. And as the power came back to normal, Chloe stopped barking. And in that silence, with Chloe wagging her tale, Barb and I just looked at each other in utter astonishment.

17
Jung: THE MISSING MOSAICS

The Galla Placidia Mausoleum in Italy is a Roman structure built around 430 AD and known for its beautiful mosaics. Carl Jung visited the place twice in his life.

On the first visit in 1913, Jung enjoyed his time there but felt strange for some reason he couldn't put his finger on. End of that story.

The second visit occurred in 1933 when Jung went there with a friend. The same feeling of unease slid over him, but again, he found no reason for it. As if that weren't enough though, he noticed a blue light in one room that seemed to have no source. Brushing both incidents aside, he went on to enjoy his tour of the mausoleum.

As Jung and his friend entered another room, they saw four very attractive biblical mosaics where Jung had seen *windows* on his first visit. Realizing he must have missed those particular panels back in 1913, he began to question his memory. Even so, the two people stood there studying the newly found pieces of art and talked about them for twenty minutes.

After leaving the mausoleum, Jung went to a store in order to buy picture post cards of those mosaics to take home with him. Sadly, he couldn't find any and no one seemed to know what he was talking about.

So impressed was Jung with those four mosaics, he even mentioned them in some of his lectures after he returned home.

Sometime later, he asked a friend who was planning a trip to Italy, and visiting the Galla Placidia Mausoleum, to buy him the post cards he couldn't find. The friend agreed, but upon return from his travels, he told Jung that he was unable to find any such panels at the mausoleum. Instead, the man found only the windows Jung had originally seen there in 1913. And, of course, since no such mosaics existed, he too was unable to buy postcards of them.

In writing about this experience many years later, Jung still marveled about it and said that the memory of those four mosaics continued to burn brightly in his mind. Did they exist there at some point in time? He never found out.

Section 3

Psychics, Mediums, Dreams and Connectivity Beyond

18
Jung: THE WEDDING

One day, Carl Jung was attending a wedding at a hotel. He didn't know the bride or her family. They were his wife's friends.

At dinner, he sat opposite a bearded man who was a lawyer. The two had a nice conversation that centered on criminal psychology. When the bearded man asked him a very specific question, Jung elaborated on the point he wanted to make by adding in a lot of imagined items just as illustration. As he continued to talk though, Jung noticed how his dinner companion's expression completely changed. In fact, the other guests noticed something was wrong enough for the entire table to fall silent. Embarrassed, but not knowing what he had said to cause such a huge problem, Jung also stopped speaking.

After dessert, Jung quickly excused himself and went into the hotel lobby. There he lit a cigar and thought about what had happened at the table. Soon, another dinner guest came out and asked him why he had insulted the bearded lawyer. Insulted? Jung was flabbergasted at the accusation.

It turned out that the extra details Jung had added in his response were an exact replica of the man's life–very personal information. At that point, Jung realized he could not remember a single thing he had said to the bearded gentleman. Even years later, when writing about the event, he still couldn't recall the details of that conversation.

19
The Cassadaga Medium

In Chapter 1 of our book, *An Explosion of Being*, my wife Barbara and I tell about our fascinating encounter with a Medium. I reproduced it here in its entirety because that story gives a very close look at an initial effort by two people seeking some of life's answers. This initial part of the book comes from Barb's perspective:

"THE SPIRITUALIST COMMUNITY of Cassadaga, Florida lies just thirty miles or so from our home. While most of the Sunshine State is notoriously flat, the hills and winding roads surrounding that tiny hamlet give it the quaint appearance of having been transplanted directly from the New England countryside.

"The homes are older, but unlike their counterparts in New England, many sprout signs advertising the certified mediumistic abilities of the residents. Our decision to visit Cassadaga had been prompted by a developing need to investigate the phenomena of 'spirit communication' first-hand. Supposedly, the local mediums could see beyond the physical world in ways that might help us in the widening search for answers to our spiritual puzzle.

"It was early afternoon on a cold October day in 1977 when we parked the car in front of a small house with a little screened porch. Doug's mom, Muriel, had been there before, and had returned to Orlando amazed at the accurate information given by the medium, Mae Graves Ward.

"Spurred by Muriel's positive reaction, as well as by our intensifying desire to go beyond an academic approach to psychic investigation, Doug and I decided to have a go at a reading by an honest-to-goodness Spiritualist. What could we lose?

"Mae Ward came to the door and asked if we were the two o'clock appointment. After introducing ourselves, Doug and I were ushered around the porch to a side room where the readings were given. Mae is no youngster, but maintains a tremendous sharpness of wit. Her personal opinions are strongly stated, but with humor and honest conviction.

"With a fifty-year involvement in the Spiritualist movement, she had numerous stories. Explaining how she once had rankled a group of visitors with an accurate description of a very personal situation, Mae raised her voice with a warm laugh and said, 'Hell, if they didn't want to know things, why did they ask?'

"It seemed strange sitting there with this obviously good-natured woman, wondering if indeed she had a special linkage to the world of spirit or if she was simply a clever fraud. Could she see and hear things in that room that actually existed beyond the normal senses, or did she live with a series of daily hallucinations? Whatever the answers, our doubts left us with feelings of uneasy anticipation and some discomfort.

"As the initial small talk continued, Mae's breathing became labored, and a cough shook her body. My immediate thoughts were that this session just might be cut short. It was becoming difficult for her to communicate, when suddenly in a clear voice she asked, 'Do you know anyone who died of a chest ailment? I feel someone very close to you who was unable to breathe.'

"Doug sat bolt upright and stammered that his grandfather had passed away in just that manner many years ago. Continuing rapidly, Mae pointed to Doug and indicated that his grandfather was with us, and that he wanted Doug to know how proud he was of the work that Doug was doing.

"Then, holding up her hand, Mae said that she could see Doug's grandfather holding up his hand and pointing to his Masonic ring. 'He's letting me know that you come from a good family,' Mae said nodding toward Doug.

"Without allowing us time to react, Mae kept the perceptions rolling at an incredible rate. Not hesitating for a moment, she described the intensive care unit at the Orlando Naval Hospital where Doug's father had died. Supposedly in communication with Doug's father, Walt, at that point, Mae explained that he too was proud of the work that Doug was doing.

"Intrigued, Mae asked if he, Doug, was a teacher. When Doug answered, 'Yes,' Mae explained that somehow she saw his students as being big, like adults. Of course the description was perfect, since Doug was working only with adults in his capacity as the training director for Orange County Public School in Orlando.

"Swinging her attention to me, Mae asked if I knew Henry. I could hardly believe her words. My great-uncle, Henry, had died just weeks before, and here was this woman giving me a message of greeting from him.

"As if that weren't enough, she went on to describe the number, ages and sexes of our children. Then, quizzically, Mae looked at me and said, 'I see medicine all around you.' With my father, cousin, grandfather, great-grandfather, and four great uncles all physicians, I could only agree that her visions were quite correct.

"She now asked both of us, 'Do you know William?' Mae went on to explain that Doug's father was telling her that he had brought William with him. We were both puzzled until Doug, remembering, said, 'Of course, William was Dad's father (Doug's other grandfather). He died when I was a year old. I never knew him.'

"At her usual breakneck speed, Mae then explained, 'Doug, your father says that your brother isn't doing too well. Is something wrong with his head? Your dad says that he spends a lot of time near your brother and that sometimes he wishes your brother could join 'them' on the other side. Now, why would he say that?' My heart went out to Doug.

"His admission that, recently, his severely mentally handicapped brother had been near death on more than one occasion must have cut through him like a knife. Doug's depth of feeling for his brother usually remains unstated, but his eyes and the silence that surrounds the subject tell a story all their own.

"On and on went the intonation from Mae Ward. Most of it made perfect sense with only small portions that didn't seem to fit. Finally, the session came close to ending with Mae saying, "Well, I don't see any big problems with you kids. Things will be even better in three years. I see you two selling your house, and Doug, I see you changing jobs. Yes, a step up in fact. I see you selling something, Doug." Now, that was a laugh. The last thing in the world Doug would be involved in would be sales.

"As we stood up to go, Mae stopped me and said, 'Lettie says to take good care of that little girl (referring to our daughter, Nicole). She says especially to keep her out of drafts and to watch out for her ears. There's some problem in that area. Oh, and also you've got a clock that isn't working. Look for it to start again soon.' With that final admonition, we bid goodbye to a very interesting lady and began our short trek back to Orlando.

" 'Who is Lettie?' " Doug asked as he started the car.

" 'Lettie was my grandmother,' " I replied, " 'Grandpa Hill's wife who died in 1955.' "

"Two years after that brief conversation, we would have cause to remember the words of caution from Lettie when Nicole developed a chronic ear infection that eventually led to surgery. Mae Ward had been a virtual whirlwind of surprise information.

"The first few minutes while being back on the road were very quiet as our minds tried to adjust to all that had occurred. Finally, Doug broke the silence to ask if I had given Mae our names, phone number or address when I made the appointment over the phone. I reminded him that Mae had not asked for any information.

"Obviously, he was referring to the history of certain fraudulent practices whereby fake mediums carefully research their clients ahead of time and charge exorbitant fees for their services. In this case though, there was absolutely no way that Mae could have researched us. Even if it had been possible, the time and effort required to find out such detailed information would have far outweighed the small amount of money that we literally had to press upon Mae at the end of our session.

"Then again, we could have been witnessing a classic example of telepathy. Doug's reading on that subject had left him halfway convinced that Mae could have been picking information out of our conscious minds, genuinely believing that she was in touch with a spirit world.

"Suddenly, Doug remembered that his grandfather's Masonic ring lay carefully packed away in a box at home. Even with telepathy, how could Mae have seen something that Doug had forgotten?

"Perhaps as another theory goes, telepathy might be a subconscious activity as well. Then again, even if we had been witnessing telepathy that in itself moved our understanding of communication into a new and exciting realm.

"The many notes that Doug took during our trip to Cassadaga were carefully rewritten and filed away for future reference. It was obvious that going beyond the telepathic explanation could be done only by validating some of Mae's predictions. If future events were to occur as she had said, then perhaps some other phenomenon was at work. In fact, this didn't take long.

"One day, a few weeks later, an old wall clock that had refused to run suddenly sprang to life and kept perfect time for two years. It would be three years, however, before verification of the other predictions came about."

The medium, Mae Graves Ward, died many years ago, but her gifts to Barb and me will last forever. A fascinating coincidence relating to this wonderful woman involves her home. See the following chapter.

20
The Cassadaga Connections

In our investigations into the paranormal, my wife Barbara and I have come to the conclusion that no events are truly coincidental. Having that belief is one thing, but seeing it demonstrated in a highly dramatic way tends to really grab your attention.

This is the recent story about such a happening.

The book Barb and I wrote about the paranormal was originally published by an imprint of Prentice Hall back in 1984. When we brought *An Explosion of Being* back to life through my company, Old St. Augustine Publications, in the fall of 2011, I began to wonder about the people who read that first edition. Did the book have any lasting effect on them? Did anyone actually keep a copy or did they just give it away? Questions like that.

Two days later, the phone rang. The caller ID said, "Cassadaga Camp." Cassadaga? Barb and I hadn't had any actual connection with that Spiritualist town just north of us since we went there for a psychic reading in 1979. In our book, we wrote about our visit to Cassadaga and the medium, Mae Graves Ward, but I couldn't see how this phone call could relate to that in any way. Much to my amazement, I soon discovered how wrong I was.

It turned out that the caller, was Selene Green, the manager for the Cassadaga Camp Bookstore and IInformation Center. This is what she said: "You probably don't remember me, but I was the manager of the B. Dalton's bookstore in Gainesville,

Florida when you and your wife did a book signing there back in 1985." She went on to say that she still had her copy of our book we signed for her at the time, and she believed that it led her to her present position in Cassadaga.

To say I was astounded doesn't begin to explain how I felt. Before I had time to recover though, Selene put another woman on the phone. "Hi Doug, I'm an old friend of your wife and I hired her to work in the Seminole County Chamber of Commerce back in 1985."

My phone connection with Cassadaga was getting weirder by the moment. This woman's name rang a bell in my startled brain and Barb had indeed worked at the Seminole County Chamber.

"I know you won't believe this," Barb's friend went on to say, "but I'm living in Mae Graves Ward's house here in Cassadaga, the medium you and Barb visited."

What a double-barreled surprise! Talk about getting your questions answered and making a point about there being no coincidences! A few weeks after that phone conversation, Barb and I went to Cassadaga and had dinner with both Selene and Barb's friend. We had a wonderful time catching up on the intervening years, talking about what brought us all together again, and discussing the paranormal.

21
A Visit in the Night

Dreams and their connection to other realms. That's what this posting is about and it comes to you from a trusted guest blogger. This person, who will remain anonymous, is very analytical and never accepts things on face value. Here's his story:

In my dream, I was approached by a woman in some non-distinct place, other than that the light was very dim, almost like a candlelight supper.

I knew she looked familiar, but couldn't make out her face until she came to a stop right in front of me.

That was when I realized she looked familiar because she was my grandmother, who had succumbed to cancer back in the mid 90's while I was in the navy and out to sea for 6 months, so I never had the chance to see her in her final days, or go to her funeral.

Gram was just simply gone when I got back for some leave time.

Anyway, the gram I was face to face with now was a beautiful young woman and just beaming with love. We embraced in a hug, she then held me out at arm's length, and told me psychically "just LOOK at how well you're doing!"

With that, she gave me the biggest kiss on the cheek you can imagine, and it was over.

For me it was a no brainer that this was a direct encounter, especially being that during this particular period of time

I had been having numerous lucid dreams and out-of-body experiences.

What was the purpose? Dunno. Maybe sometimes these events happen just for the sake of them happening. The images and feelings to be stored in the bank of our subconscious of things that we now "know" are real, and don't have to believe or take anyone else's word for any more. Maybe they're the well timed and needed encouragement we all need from time to time on this tough road of Samsara we trod together. Or, maybe she just wanted to say hello...LOL. Maybe all three, or more.

What I DO know is there are infinite realms of existence beyond our nearly blind 5 physical senses, that we are a part of them, they are a part of us, and by birthright we are free to explore them if we so choose. All of us.

22
The Portal

Guest post by my friend, ghost hunter and Florida author about things paranormal, Dave Lapham:

A friend the other day read "Gateway to Hell" in my book *Ghosts of St. Augustine* and asked me about portals, if they really existed. I have witnessed a portal. My wife, Sue, and I visited Ireland a few years ago and went to Clonmacnoise, a religious center established around 545 A.D. at the crossroads of the River Shannon and the glacial ridge running across Ireland.

We were standing in a cold rain amid the ruins of an old chapel, praying for a friend suffering from a brain tumor. As we stood there, something opened in front of us and enveloped us. It was hard to describe. It wasn't so much that we walked through a doorway, but rather that the doorway surrounded us as we stood. We were not frightened, but we were overwhelmed with a peaceful, joyful sensation.

This cocoon-like feeling lasted for several minutes, then dissipated, leaving both of us exhilarated, overjoyed, and energized. The experience was the most astounding thing that's ever happened to me. I know many others who have also experienced portals, among them my friend, Melba Goodwyn. She devotes an entire chapter to the subject in her book, *Ghost Worlds*.

"The Spanish Washer Woman" in my book, *Ancient City Hauntings*, is another dramatic story about a portal.

We know that many dimensions exist other than the one we live in. Some believe there are infinite numbers of such things floating around the universe. We also know that not all of these dimensions are parallel, and where they intersect you will find a portal. The Irish call them "thin places." Melba defines them as inter-dimensional doorways opening into other realms of existence. As dimensions are not always fixed, so portals aren't either, although some can last a very long time.

Portals can appear almost anywhere, inside structures or outside. They are often found in cemeteries, I guess, because consciously or subconsciously, we choose burial grounds for their otherworldly characteristics, spiritual vibrations, or auras. Cemeteries often innately exhibit sacredness and peace and where portals are often found. But portals may also appear under more negative circumstances and can be anything but peaceful.

In her book, Melba explains that we can discern energy patterns which might indicate the presence of a portal. These energy patterns, especially noticeable to people who are sensitive to such things, can be either harmonious or discordant. One can experience peace, euphoria, increased energy, elation, calmness. Or the energies cause weakness, nausea, headaches, cold chills, confusion.

There are other common signs. You may hear barely audible humming or buzzing, feel static electricity, or see orb-like forms streaking around. The light around a portal may also seem either unnaturally bright or shaded, inconsistent with its surroundings. And there may be mist or fog concentrated in the area.

In any case, if you ever experience or think you are experiencing a portal, be careful. It may be a calming, peaceful place, or it may be something evil—as in my "Gateway to Hell" story. Either way, experiencing a portal is going to change your thinking about time and space.

23
Dreaming of Russia

Reincarnation? Can you dream about past lives? The follow-ing came from my dream journal written many years ago:

I was in Russia, somewhere in the early nineteen hundreds. I could feel the bitter cold through the heavy clothing I wore.

Snow covered the streets where I was standing. The day was dark, as if again, it was about to snow. The building in front of me, and those up and down the streets, appeared massive and grey in the gloom

My comrade lay crumpled at my feet, dead from a hail of bullets. I knelt before his body. The snow crunched beneath my knees. The firing squad was behind me. I knew that I would be executed also.

Seconds later, the rifles exploded, ripping through my body, tearing my lungs apart. Strangely, there was no pain. With total serenity, I toppled over my friend to join him in death.

Then, almost as an observer of the entire scene, I casually realized how the shredding of my lungs by those bullets, in that lifetime, was a direct cause of recurring asthma in my childhood this lifetime.

Since my dream seemed so very real, I eventually went to the library to see if I could find anything that might match what I experienced. It didn't take long. Amazingly, I discovered a photo of the initial stages of the Russian Revolution in St. Petersburg that looked almost identical to my dream environment. It gave me chills looking at that thing. When I found it, I tried to reason it away because I always liked Russian history. "Just a little creative nighttime tinkering with something you like," I told myself. But the shiver that ran up and down my spine when I first looked at that photo still gives me that same reaction when I when I view it now.

Historical Background: Russian workers and religious leaders trying to serve a petition to Czar Nicholas were gunned down in the square in front of the Winter Place. At least 100 people died and many more were injured. The year was 1905 and the event became known as Bloody Sunday.

Did I actually live and die back then? I don't know, of course, but I tend to think that's a good possibility.

24
Dream Communications

The following paranormal dream event I had a number of years ago comes directly from the book my wife Barbara and I wrote titled, *An Explosion of Being*:

"I awoke in the middle of the night, almost capturing all of a very colorful and active dream. As I edged back into sleep, suddenly, I was facing what appeared to be the muted colors of several very symmetrical, molecular-type structures.

"Each of those things looked much like the patterns visible through a child's kaleidoscope. The contrast to the previous dream's color and fast-paced action was surprising, especially since there was no movement or sound of any kind.

"Still close to consciousness, I woke myself, vaguely sensing that something important was happening. But tiredness won out. As the last drops of awareness faded back into sleep, the kaleidoscope images flickered briefly into view. This phenomena recurred randomly during other nights over the next several years. Each time, the encounter began in the dream state, flowing over, eventually, into a waking consciousness.

"This repetitious event never varied and was consistently monotonous. But, the continual reappearance and visual clarity of those images seemed to be forming a comfort based on familiarity.

"No, it was more than that. It was almost as if I had always known the meaning of those structures and was slowly uncovering that knowledge, layer by layer.

"In May of that year, my daughter Nicole was still young enough to take afternoon naps. One rainy Sunday, as a dutiful father, I stretched out with her to insure drowsiness. Soon, according to Barb anyway, I was snoring while Nicole happily played with her stuffed animals.

"In that short span of slumber, I again encountered those familiar geometric shapes. This occurrence, in itself, isn't noteworthy except for its direct connection to a later, more important event.

"What happened during the early morning hours after I went to sleep that same night was so forceful, I had to get out of bed and enter that experience in my dream journal:

May 26, 2:50 AM

"Got to sleep about midnight. Extensive dreaming. In one particular dream, Nicole was calling me. She needed help or assistance of some kind. Soon, she ran to me and threw her arms around my neck.

"At this point, I awakened. I could hear thunder and raindrops beginning to fall on the plants outside the window. I realized then that our storm from the evening before was returning. Didn't open my eyes, but when I was about to, a voice in my mind said, 'Just relax and enjoy the storm in a different way.'

"Immediately, my body calmed with an unusual thoroughness. I, or the essence of me, was almost detached from that relaxed flesh. My mind then became filled with visions of beautiful patterns of color.

"These patterns would ebb and flow, brighten and change. How wonderful! I was maintaining full consciousness and prolonging a view of something that I had seen only in snatches during previous dream conditions (the geometrical, molecular structures).

"The color patterns then changed to a magnificent panorama of textured greens, containing minute particles of varied color. Vibrations seemingly emanated from each particle. The whole mass appeared to shift and rotate. The depth of this sight began to fluctuate as I sensed that now, I was seeing the 'true' sense of color, and perhaps the core of the children's book I was writing for Nicole.

"Suddenly, my mind was partially filled with a finely textured white light. It gave me a feeling of warmth and expanded my internal perceptions to a much greater degree. I had the distinct sensation of some sort of intelligence trying to contact me. Chills ran up and down my body as I then responded by reaching out for more communication through my mind.

"The patterns of color returned, but there was a noticeable difference. They were tighter, almost spherical in shape, with much finer color hues. The words came to me, 'you must begin to fully understand these things if you are to grow and progress.'

"With that statement, the spheres of patterned texture actually pulsated outward toward me and seemed to penetrate my being with the understanding.

"My consciousness of the thunder returned. As a gentle, long rumble bounced in the distance, thoughts of the children's books for Nicole sprang to mind. Then, I truly understood this pulsating communication I was experiencing was related to all of the books Barb and I would ever write.

"I opened my eyes and looked at the clock. 2: 15 AM. Lightning was flashing through the window, and I thought of Nicole. Before going to bed, she opened her curtains to watch the storm and made me promise to keep the curtains in our room open for us to do the same.

"I wondered if she, in some way, had helped to awaken me with the original dream so that I would have this experience and see the lightning as well.

"For some reason, seemingly apart from my consciousness, I sent her this mental message: 'I saw the lightning as you wanted, and I do remember the old days.' Old days? What the hell was that and where did it come from? When Nicole and I took a nap yesterday afternoon, I had seen the patterns of color. Was there a communication between Nikki and me at that time as well? Was there some sort of reincarnation related link between us?

"It's been over a half hour since I've been up. The compulsion to record this material and imprint it on my conscious mind is incredible. I still have chills.

"Sharing those notes with Barb the next day reminded me of the brilliant clarity of that experience, but beyond the recorded words was a depth of feeling that I found very difficult to describe.

"Something penetrated my being during those early morning hours in a way that I could sense, but not explain. It was almost a physical realization captured within.

"Even so, direct contact was the one inescapable conclusion that kept filtering out of my feelings, but contact with what, or whom? The geometric forms and those vibrant colors felt so alive. When they swirled towards me, I was literally engulfed by physical sensation, non-verbal communication, love and warmth.

"Neither Barb nor I were able to precisely define the nature of my contact. It did seem to be a natural outgrowth of our other communication with alternate realities, however, so we left it at that.

"For the next couple of years, I would awaken during the night from time to time to see the now familiar visions, then drift back to sleep in the midst of a very comforting, but indistinct exchange. It tended to become a random ritual, bringing with it each time, a very peaceful sense of ease."

Section 4

Ghosts, Visitations, Visions and Out-of-Body Experiences

25
Jung: GHOST VISITORS

One day in 1916, Carl Jung felt restless. He also had the strange feeling that unseen entities were in his house, but he could discover no reason for that odd conclusion.

Later in the day, one of his daughters claimed she saw an indistinct, white figure pass in front of her.

That night two of Jung's other children had these frightening experiences:

1. Somehow, another of Jung's daughters had her bed covers pulled off her. She hadn't been told of her sisters' ghostly sighting that afternoon.

2. Jung's nine-year-old son had a very bad dream about the devil.

The following day, both children told their parents about those experiences. But instead of talking about his dream, Jung's son asked for crayons, which he rarely used. Using the crayons, he drew a picture of what he remembered, which finally allowed him to explain it as follows:

- He saw a man fishing near a river.

- Somehow the man had the fishing rod attached to his head

- Nearby, a chimney spouted flames and belched smoke

- The man caught a fish

- When he caught the fish, the devil came flying out of the woods

- The devil swore at the man for stealing his fish

- Then an angel appeared

- The angel told the devil to leave the man alone because he only catches bad fish

At about 5:00 PM on that same day, the doorbell started ringing and ringing as if someone was very impatient. Jung could actually see the bell inside the house moving as well as hearing the noise.

Since it was a nice summer day and the windows were open, Jung poked his head out of one that was close to the front door. Immediately, the ringing stopped, but there was no one at the door.

Jung then had a distinct feeling something else was going to happen and it did. To him, the air in his house felt thick and crowded, as if there were a great many people everywhere.

Finally, ghostly images began speaking to him pressuring Jung to write. And write he did, for three straight evenings. He realized exactly what it was the ghostly visitors wanted him to produce. When he had completed his work, the barrage of paranormal events stopped.

What Jung wrote was something called, "The Seven Sermons of the Dead." Eventually, he included it in his famous book titled, *Memories, Dreams and Reflections.*

26
Nicole on the Bed

O nce again, this story comes from the *An Explosion of Being*, the book my wife Barb and I wrote. It is actually two events in one as told from Barb's perspective, but I experienced them as well, on more than one occasion:

Event # 1:

"While sleeping, I somehow felt and heard my daughter, Nicole, (she was age three at the time) come into our room.

"Upon waking, I thought that she needed my help or that she was sick. At that point, I could feel her move onto the bottom of the bed and crawl up toward me, which she often did. Her little hands pressed against my left foot and leg on her way up.

"Just as I was about to turn over, I felt her blowing in my ear. It was a very irritating and steady stream of air that annoyed me considerably. Ready to pounce on my sweet daughter for playing games so late at night, I found to my horror that I absolutely could not move.

"There I lay, paralyzed, with my eyes wide open, frozen in place. The blowing continued until I finally mustered all of my strength and was able to force myself to sit up. The blowing stopped.

"Nicole was nowhere to be seen. Doug was fast asleep with his back to me. "Within a few seconds, Nicole awakened in her bedroom and called to me. Until I actually saw her in bed, with the covers still in place, could I believe that she hadn't physically been in our room at all.

Event # 2:

"It was that kind of awakening which instantly transports you from the deepest sleep to the absolute clarity of consciousness. I didn't move, but lay there wondering what could have roused me so completely.

"The gentle bubbling of the fish tank in the living room was the only sound, but there was still a sense of expectancy. Nothing happened, but something was definitely about to happen. That's what it was. I could feel it hanging heavily in the air, as if it would drop any minute.

"Lying there in the darkness, I analyzed the sensation of expectancy for an instant before the familiarity hit me. On those occasions at night, when I could feel Nicole on the bed in an out-of-body condition, the sensation that preceded each encounter was the same as I was feeling at that moment.

"Within seconds, light footsteps on the carpet stopped at the foot of the bed. O.K., I thought, are you really there, or are you flitting around again, out-of-body?

"With that, my arm began to tingle. It was as if a physical imprint were purposely being made, but why? Again, within seconds, Nicole started to cry in her room. Jumping out of bed, I found her feverish and coughing. Then things began to make sense. As our channeled source told us, when Nicole can't get to us physically, she will do it in spirit."

27
Out-of-Body

Some members of my family have had very clear out-of-body experiences over the years. Me? There have been a lot of times I felt I was floating, but that's about it. Well, except for one particular night. I hesitate to mention it because what happened was so quick and very strange.

Then again, the oddity of it eventually told me that I wasn't asleep.

On the night in question, I slowly awoke out of a whole bunch of dreams. What they were, I have no idea and probably didn't even recall them at the time. It was one of those times when you are barely awake but your head is full of indistinct activity that seemed to have been happening just seconds before.

When I finally open my eyes a bit, I felt a little disoriented so I figured part of my brain must still be in the dreaming state. The darkness around me seemed very different somehow, but I just couldn't seem to pull my consciousness together enough in order to make sense of my environment. I was lying on my back, that much I knew, and nothing more. Looking straight above me, I saw rough, pebbly shapes surrounding some sort of rectangular object.

In the gloom, I stared at the thing in the ceiling for the longest time trying to figure it out. Slowly, it dawned on me that I was looking at an air conditioning vent set into the ceiling—all that rough, pebbly stuff that I first noticed.

The more I stared, the clearer the vent became. In fact, I was able to actually look inside the thing and inspect it in infinite detail.

This all seemed vaguely interesting until it hit me that the only way I could be seeing the inside of the vent would be if I was lying parallel to the ceiling with my face only inches from it— and using a flashlight.

Impossible, I finally realized with a start. The vent is 8 feet high and 6 feet from the bed. Wide-eyed, I stared at the close-up scene directly in front of my eyes for a few more seconds before I suddenly found myself in bed, lying on my back.

Barb was sleeping soundly next to me, and the room was mostly dark, as it should have been. Turning my head to the left, I looked for the vent and found it just barely visible way up there on the ceiling, where I knew without a doubt I had just been.

28
A Ghost Story with a Twist

Before and during the time that my wife Barbara and I were writing our paranormal nonfiction book, *An Explosion of Being*, we were involved in an extensive amount of channeling.

Barb was the link while I simply asked questions and took notes.

During one of those sessions, I noticed an ill-defined shape, grey in color, near where I sat. Roughly the size of a person standing, it only hung there in the air for a few seconds before disappearing.

I have to admit, that appearance startled me a little, but it was of such short duration, I wondered if I imagined/hallucinated it. The only other logical explanation was that we had briefly been visited by a ghost. Perfectly reasonable conclusions, right? Wrong. Well, in a way.

When Barb finished delivering the channeled information to a previously asked question, I decided to query her about what I had just seen.

"You saw what?" She asked with her eyes still closed as she sat in her recliner.

Again, I explained my vision and requested she ask for information. By that time in our paranormal explorations, we broadly identified the *source* of Barb's channeled communications simply as *The Source* and left it at that without trying to refine it any more. *The* Source often identified itself mysteriously as "we."

What I saw, The Source told us, was Barb's mother, Virginia, who was quite alive and well at the time. She lived just a few miles away. It seems, according to The Source, that Virginia was asleep at the time of our channeling session. And as she slept, she had gone spirit traveling and ended up at our house. Or at least we were on her visitation list. It seems that she was simply curious about what we were doing.

Interesting, huh? That event and resulting communication made us wonder how many ghost encounters might actual be such out-of-body experiences.

29
A Pegasus in Orlando?

The following story is from my dear friend, Betty Howe. She writes about a very strange but wondrous experience.

I got to know this delightful lady many years ago when we both worked as school administrators here in the Central Florida area. Betty is one of the most intelligent, sober, honest, levelheaded, and no-nonsense people I know. That's what makes her story all the more alluring.

Sadly though, my good friend, Betty, died in January of 2015. For her Christmas present, I had given her a review copy of this book so that she could see her story. She is greatly missed.

I've only shared this story with family members and a few close friends. Most people would not have believed me anyway and others would have thought I was crazy, drunk or hallucinating.

It happened on a beautiful, spring day in a huge nature preserve east of Orlando. After checking with the park ranger, my traveling companion and I drove as far as we could, parked the car where the road ended, and used a picnic table to grab a quick bite of lunch. There was no one else around—just nature and us.

When we finished our meal, we began our exploration of the surrounding area. Eventually, though, my friend and I ventured off in different directions. She was soon out of sight and I started following a small stream. All that running water seemed to hold a definite attraction for me. Instead of resisting the impulse, I just gave in to it, followed the stream, and enjoyed myself immensely.

Very soon, however, everything changed. I noticed movement of some kind back in the woods on the other side of my little waterway, so I stopped dead in my tracks. Then out of the trees walked a magnificent white Pegasus making not one bit of sound. Yes, the winged horse of ancient Greek myth.

I can't explain it to you, but I felt no astonishment, fear or even curiosity. No. All I felt was peaceful acceptance of what I was observing. It just … seemed natural somehow, and I had no need to understand the event unfolding before me.

The Pegasus took no notice of me whatsoever. With its wings folded, the creature simply walked to the water's edge, lowered its head and drank from the stream. When it had had enough, it shook its head, turned around, and retreated back into the woods as quietly as it had appeared.

I offer you no explanation as to what I saw. I feel no need to do so. The only reason I'm telling this story publicly after all these years is because my friend, Doug Dillon, requested it of me. He seems to feel it might have some value and that's good enough for me.

After Betty told me this story, I went to the Internet and looked up the creature she had seen. In that search, I discovered that Pegasus is associated with natural phenomena—mainly water. Betty had no knowledge of this particular aspect of Greek mythology.

30
The Voice

What you have here is a response to an interview question posed to me about my writing and St. Augustine, Florida. The question was this: "During the times when you are in St. Augustine, and actually engaged in writing your paranormal fiction for young adults, have you ever experienced anything spooky?" Here's my answer:

To be honest, only once. And it happened right after I stopped writing one night and had gone to bed. At least I call it paranormal even if no one else does. It was in the spring of 2010. My friend Gary let me stay at his place in the city so I could start working on the second book of my young adult series, **The St. Augustine Trilogy.** Gary's house is a fairly new, three-story, poured concrete home in an extraordinarily quiet, yet historic, part of the city—perfect isolation for writing.

One evening I worked late and finally crawled into bed around 2: 00 AM. I had just dropped off to sleep when a loud voice of what sounded like a young woman said, "Hellll-loooooo." Yup, just like that.

It was as if she was standing at the foot of my bed and trying to wake me up— a friendly but unwanted greeting. Immediately, I sat bolt upright and peered into the gloom. But I couldn't see anything unusual and heard nothing more from what I still felt was a visiting presence. A little shiver ran down my spine. Strangely though, I was unafraid.

Yeah, maybe I was just dreaming, but I'll tell you one thing about that event. I can still recall being asleep, but upon hearing the voice before fully waking up, I knew without a doubt there was no one else physically in the room with me. It was as if I instantly recognized how that single word had definitely came from outside of me but originated from a nonphysical and nonthreatening source. I tried to convince myself I was only dreaming, but way down inside, I knew that wasn't the case.

31
Children's Sensitivities: Part 1

I believe that some of my earliest childhood memories are definitely paranormal in nature. In fact, as I try thinking back into the mists of my own history, those memories overshadow most other past events from ages three to five with incredible potency. Maybe that's because some of what happened was a repetition of the same type of event, possibly on a daily basis, and one which my parents continually told me wasn't real. My guess, not an exact memory, is that they told me it was a dream. Why? Because this repeating experience only happened while I was in bed, early in the morning. Makes sense, right? Kid thinks he wakes up but is actually still asleep. The thing is, even at that tender age, I knew better.

It always began right after I awakened, usually before my parents got up and when everything was still very quiet. Little objects would appear directly in front of me floating in the air. The first ones to show up were always toys of some kind, very familiar type of things.

As more of them appeared, they began to slowly move in a straight line towards the wall next to my bed. Then the line of toys in the air morphed into other things.

Those new objects were very strange, like nothing else I had encountered in my short life. They were so weird that I couldn't really describe them to my parents, nor can I adequately describe them to you now. All I can say is that they seemed to be very colorful, amorphous, circular blobs.

My memory tells me that those colors and shapes changed as I watched, but I can't make such a statement with any certainty. What I am fairly sure of though, is that those objects were still there, at times, when my parents came to roust me out of bed. When I tried to show them what I was seeing, they told me nothing was there.

Like the floating toy objects, those blobs followed the same direct, straight-line path towards the wall next to my bed. When any of the objects reached the wall, they simply went into it and disappeared. Of course, that fascinated me no end. Although both toys and blobs looked solid, they could somehow penetrate another solid object. Knowing those weird objects had to be solid, I always tried to grab or pinch them but never succeeded. My fingers just went right through toys and blobs alike.

Very frustrating, but after a while it became a fun game until my parents arose. As soon as I got out of bed and started my day, all the objects vanished.

Dreams? Imagination? Hallucinations? That's what I thought well into my adulthood until I started studying the paranormal. For such a long time, I bought my parents' explanations. But that all changed when other experiences and research helped me to understand how what we call reality can have many levels, usually unseen.

When my wife Barbara and I wrote our book, *An Explosion of Being: An American Family's Journey into the Psychic* many years ago, we created a chapter titled, "Children-Colleagues in Awareness." We did so hoping parents and other family members who read it might take children's unusual experiences a little more seriously. If that happens, we think children will feel more validated and perhaps everyone will learn just a bit more about what is means to be alive in this reality. We raised our kids in such a way, and they are happy we did.

In closing, I want to mention one more thing. In thinking about writing this posting, it suddenly struck me that there might well be a connection between the little blobs I saw as a child and experiences much later in my adulthood.

While writing *An Explosion of Being*, I had numerous vivid dreams where beautiful molecular structures were somehow communicating with me without using words.

Eventually, this led to extremely intense dream sequences where I became something like a bursting firework. This was followed by what I can only describe as a tremendous explosion that shook the house and started me awake. No one else awoke. It was as if the explosion was meant only for me. From that event came the title of our book, *An Explosion of Being*.

The point of that story is this. I now wonder if my little, colorful, childhood blobs were related to those beautiful, communicating, geometric structures I encountered many decades later. Did they provide a mental construct over time that allowed for more in-depth communication to occur later in life? Interesting question isn't it?

32
Children's Sensitivities: Part 2

As I wrote in a previous post (the last chapter), somewhere between the ages of three and five, I saw mysterious blobs of patterned color every morning when I awoke. Those blobs looked solid, but I was unable to touch them and they disappeared by entering the wall next to my bed.

I mention those events because I now believe them to have been paranormal in nature and they laid a base for the next three short stories.

It seems to me, you see, some of my early childhood memories, like the one above, tell me that I had certain sensitivities. The next three stories support that notion and demonstrate how parents and society in general can force a child to abandon their natural abilities to perceive beyond the norm. I don't blame my parents for their part in this, but it is a fact that after the next three events, to my knowledge, I didn't have another paranormal experience until I was in my thirties.

To my younger readers, I suggest you hold onto your hats because we are now going way back in time to when I was six-years-old. To be specific, 1949. Yes, believe it or not, someone who lived in the mid twentieth century can still be alive—at this writing in 2012 anyway.

In early 1949, my dad was sent to Germany as part of the occupation forces stationed there after World War II. Once he got situated in his new job and found a house, he sent for my mother and me (age six).

The house he finally found was HUGE—three stories and a basement. It was fenced all around and had an electronic door just to get into our front yard. It turned out that a former Nazi owned the place and we rented it from him.

The following three events are things that happened to me shortly after our arrival:

Noises in the Night

My bedroom was right next to my parents' bedroom on the second floor. Both rooms were connected by a door my folks often left partially open before going to bed.

That first night at the house, I climbed into my new bed, early as usual. My parents left a small light on in their room so I wouldn't be scared until it was time for them to retire as well.

I wasn't frightened at all, but I just couldn't sleep. When my parents finally went to bed, they turned out all the lights, which made my room pitch dark. That was fine for a few minutes, until I started hearing something in my room.

It clearly sounded as if someone was walking around. There were rustlings, footsteps and the floorboards creaked. My parents heard none of this.

I called out to my mom and dad, assuming it had to be one of them nearby, but no such luck. From their room, they told me I was imagining things and to go to sleep.

That's when I started getting really scared.

When all that walking around continued, I screamed for my parents. Here began a long period of time with me hearing those same sounds, my parents turning on lights and assuring me in person that no one else was in the house.

Even so, I became terrified. I cried and screamed so much, my dad eventually came in and laid down the law. No more crying and screaming. Period. Understandable, I say now looking back, but it sure seemed unsympathetic at the time.

The only way I was finally able to shut the sounds out and get to sleep was to cover my head with sheets, a blanket and a pillow. I never heard those sounds again during the entire three years of our stay.

The Little City

Something else happened in my room soon after the event above, however, that gave me another good scare.

As usual, I went to bed one night before my parents did. I was lying there in the semi darkness when I had the strongest urge to look over the side of my bed. I just knew something would be there and I was right.

As soon as I looked, an entire daytime scene had spread itself across my floor. I was looking down at a little city far below me. To this day, I even recall the tile roofing on some of those buildings. Totally startled and literally afraid of falling from such a great height, I screamed bloody murder.

My parents came running up from the first floor. I don't remember how long it took them to calm me down so I could sleep, but it was a while. Never had another vision of any kind in that house.

My Dad's Death?

This was a dream event, one that was so clear and so frightening, it scared me to think about it for years afterward.

I was sitting by the edge of a very large indoor swimming pool (at the time, I didn't even know there was such a thing as in indoor pool). No one was there but me. Kind of fun having a whole pool to myself, I thought, and then I turned around.

There, lying on his back in his swim trunks, with his eyes wide-open, was my father. He stared not at me but at the ceiling high above us. Suddenly, this weird tone began building all around me until it seemed to fill every fiber of my being with terror. At that moment I realized my father was dead.

Of course I woke up screaming.

Once again, my poor parents jumped out of bed to calm me down. Only when I saw my dad in person did I accept the fact that he was still alive. They convinced me it just an odd dream and nothing to be concerned about. But for a couple of years after that, I wondered if my dream meant my father would soon die.

Conclusions

First of all, that house was very old. I don't doubt it contained something, some sort of residual energy and/or entities that activated my natural sensitivities.

On my first night there, I think I must have immediately picked up on whatever existed in my room. Even so, my parents were probably right by forcing me to shut off my ability to connect with such things. Otherwise, I might have driven myself crazy with fear. Besides, they certainly were not prepared to help me figure out what was going on.

Hmmm. Actually, we had a break-in a year or two after that. Someone entered through our kitchen on the first floor and stole a bunch of things. We all slept right through it. Maybe those noises I heard on that first night were from future events, or not.

Thankfully though, my father lived a lot longer than I thought he would as a child. Even so, he did die relatively early in life in 1975 at age fifty-seven. His final hour came at the old Orlando Naval Hospital, which was near a lake in those days. The pool from my dream? I wonder.

My little city? The only thing I can say is that later on during my stay in Germany, my parents took me traveling with them to several other European countries. Many of the small towns I saw looked very similar to my little city near the bed, tiled roofs and all.

33
Ghost Playmates: Part 1

Guest post by my friend, ghost hunter and Florida author, Dave Lapham. Most of this story occurred in St. Augustine, Florida:

Betsy knew the house was haunted when she bought it. The previous owners were candid about it. They'd told her about the little girl, Rose Marie, who had died in the back bedroom upstairs in 1837, during a typhoid epidemic.

Those previous owners told her that Rose was still there, not menacing, but present. Betsy didn't care. She didn't believe in ghosts anyway. She wanted to live in St. Augustine.

As a single mom, Betsy had struggled for several years, until a long-lost uncle left her with millions. Tired of living out in the sticks in Hastings, Florida, she turned her eye toward St. Augustine and quickly found this fine, old coquina house on Marine Street. The asking price was $950,000, a little steep perhaps, but Betsy had the money. Why not? She could afford it.

The house had been built in 1794 by Don Hector Vitorio Montalvo de Sevilla, during Spain's last possession of Florida. It was one of the oldest structures in the city. The history of St. Augustine fascinated Betsy, and she snapped up the house as soon as she saw it.

Seven-year-old Alice Sue, Betsy's daughter, loved the house, too. She ran through all the rooms, laughing, inquisitive, and instantly was drawn to the back bedroom. "This is my room,

Mommy," she shouted to her mother out in the hall. Betsy, knowing the room had once supposedly belonged to Rose Marie Slater, smiled and said, "Of course, sweetie. You can have the room."

The property was narrow but ran from Marine Street all the way over to Avenida Menendez with a wall surrounding it. The previous owners had done a wonderful job of landscaping the back garden with little nooks and crannies, vine-covered pergolas, and hideaways. Betsy thought her daughter would be enthralled by it all, but from the very first Alice Sue preferred her own room overlooking the beautiful garden.

Alice Sue loved her room because she had found a playmate there, another little girl about her age who arrived and left through the closet. Alice Sue thought that a bit odd, but the little girl was otherwise a wonderful friend.

That friend's name was Rose Marie. She told Alice Sue that her father was an American and her mother, Spanish. Her black hair and dark complexion contrasted nicely with Alice Sue's light skin and blond hair. And she didn't come just to play. Sometimes she came at night and slept with Alice Sue, because she missed her parents.

Betsy often passed by her daughter's door to hear giggling and laughing. She might have been concerned, at least enough to look in on Alice Sue, but the child had always had imaginary playmates. Betsy thought this was the case again, just an imaginary playmate. She did think about Rose Marie Slater but quickly dismissed the thought. Besides, if Rose Marie was the "imaginary" playmate, what harm was there?

This story is continued in the next chapter.

34
Ghost Playmates: Part 2

This is a continuation of the St. Augustine ghost story begun on Chapter 32 by my friend, ghost hunter and Florida author, Dave Lapham:

For Alice Sue's part she enjoyed every minute with Rose Marie. In addition to coming and going through the closet, she asked some funny questions, like "What is that thing on the table next to your bed?"

"You mean the lamp?"

"Lamp?"

"Yes. Here, I'll turn it on." Alice Sue pulled the lamp chain and the light came on.

"Oh," Rose Marie exclaimed and jumped back.

And there were the shoes. Rose Marie wore what seemed to Alice Sue old-fashioned handmade slippers. Rose Marie was astounded by Alice Sue's Skecher Twinkle Toes with its pink laces, leopard spots and lights that flashed with every step.

When Alice Sue let her friend try them on, the girl was so enthralled, she gave them to Rose Marie.

But the admiration wasn't one-sided. Alice Sue loved Rose Marie's clothes, which were so well-made and so different. One day she came out of the closet wearing what to Alice Sue was a beautiful pink dress, with ruffles all the way down to the hem, a wide pink ribbon at the waist, and little pink bows all around the scoop neck. She had to have a dress just like it.

Weeks later as Alice Sue's birthday neared, Betsy asked her daughter what she wanted. Immediately, she said, "A dress, a pink, full-length dress." And she described Rose Marie's dress in minute detail. Betsy thought it odd, but she told her that's what she'd get, and she wrote down the description Alice Sue had given her.

Alice Sue and her mother knew no one in St. Augustine, so the "birthday party" consisted of just the two of them. First, Alice Sue opened her gifts at home—and immediately put on her new dress.

The two girls then walked up the street for lunch at the Casa Monica Hotel. At the end of the meal, a waitress came out with a piece of cake, a candle burning on it, and all the wait staff sang "Happy Birthday" to Alice Sue. She laughed as she blew out the candle and ate the cake but soon was anxious to rush home.

She ran down the street ahead of her mother and was waiting at the door when Betsy arrived. Then she bounded up to her room and closed the door. Shortly after, Betsy heard squeals and giggles coming from upstairs.

When Alice Sue turned toward the closet she saw Rose Marie standing there—in her pink dress. Rose Marie's jaw dropped and she broke into a big smile. The two little girls stood looking at each other, eyes glistening. Rose Marie reached out her hand and took Alice Sue's. She led her to the closet, and the two walked in, closing the door.

Alice Sue was never seen again, but to this day one can hear two little girls giggling and laughing in the bedroom upstairs at the end of the hall in the old coquina house on Marine Street.

35
Cries in the Night

Here is the third of four events reported by my friend, Patrick Delsaut, a writer and paranormal explorer from France. This one occurred in 1989:

It was dark and all was quiet in my house and in the neighborhood. I wasn't asleep and my mind was very clear.

This event happened just as I went into a hallway where the stairs led to the bedrooms. That's when I thought I heard something. So I stopped breathing to listen better and, indeed, sounds were coming from above. Slowly, I walked to the foot of the stairs.

When I got there, I heard something I never wanted to hear—little plaintive cries coming from my father's old bedroom. He had died in 1987. That was the same bedroom where, years before, my mother, sister and I had heard strange footsteps.

Icy chills invaded my body. Something told me to save myself, but I wanted to be sure I was not dreaming. So I stayed at the bottom of the stairs alone, shivering and listening to those horrible cries.

No, I was not dreaming. Those chilling sounds were coming out of my late father's room and they were not coming from his ghost.

I say chilling, because those plaintive cries were not human or animal. They were both sweet and powerful, lightweight and violent, bass and treble— a wild and weird mixture I had never heard before. I became very afraid.

In fact, I was so scared that I did not go up the stairs and look in my father's old room. No, I felt much too much negativity coming from those sounds to explore the situation any further. The negativity seemed so strong I would even call it evil.

At the height of my fear, the cries suddenly stopped and I never heard them again.

36
The Ghostly Farewell

This is the last of four events reported by my friend, Patrick Delsaut, a writer and paranormal explorer from France. This one took place in 1994:

Night had long since fallen and I was washing before going to bed. All of a sudden, when everything was calm and quiet, I experienced something that had never happened to me before.

I heard a crystalline voice, but it was inside my head. Even though I didn't hear it through my ears, that voice was even clearer than if it had been spoken aloud. The feeling was really very special, very strange.

This voice said only three words: "Are you there"? That little sentence was heavy with meaning for me because it was something Lucette, my sister's best friend, always said. Lucette had just died of septicemia after a kidney transplant.

There is no doubt in my mind, my sister's friend came to tell me goodbye in her own way before ascending to heaven on the astral plane. But why me and not my sister? She was her friend?

I believe it was simply because she felt my connection to the sensitive spheres of beyond. I could hear her telepathic message while my sister could not. Lucette knew that I would hear her farewell words and I did.

37
The Last Goodbye

Continuing the thread from the previous chapter, one that humankind has repeatedly echoed, I want to tell you about my great-grandparents on my mother's side of the family. Born in the late 1800's, they were a very devoted couple who spent a lifetime together.

My grandmother told me this quick story, one she experienced herself. So, just to clarify, this is about her parents. She said she stayed with her father in his home when her mother, my great-grandmother, fell ill and went to the hospital:

Well before dawn, she awoke to find my great-grandfather also awake and very agitated. He told her his wife, my great-grandmother, had entered their bedroom and said goodbye to him.

It took some time, but my grandmother finally got her father calmed down and convinced him he had been dreaming. Then the phone rang. The hospital called with the news my great-grandmother had died.

This story rang so true for me over the years that I used a similar one in my young adult books titled, *Sliding Beneath the Surface*. Truth is not only stranger than fiction, it can also lay a very firm basis for the fiction we create.

Do you have such stories in your family history? If so, write them down so they won't be lost.

Section 5

Coincidences and Synchronicity

38
Jung: THE SCARAB BEETLE

One of Carl Jung's patients was a young woman, very educated and intelligent, who seemed to feel she knew more than anyone else about everything, including her therapist. This proved problematic, obviously, because Jung couldn't get through to her even after multiple sessions.

Finally, he realized that the woman would never listen to him or solve her problems unless something highly unusual shook her world enough to dislodge her sense of superiority. What that might be, he had no idea.

During their next session together in Jung's office, he sat opposite the woman with his back to a window. As usual, she rattled on, this time about a dream she had the night before. She told Jung that in the dream someone gave her a gold scarab.

While the woman was speaking, Jung kept hearing something hitting the window behind him. The sound continued even after the woman stopped talking, so Jung turned around to look. What he saw was a large bug. It kept bumping the window as if trying to get in.

Jung thought it strange enough that he got up, walked to window and opened it. Somehow he caught the bug and then recognized it as a type of scarab beetle. Realizing he might have something unusual enough to truly grab the woman's attention, he brought her the beetle and said, "Here is your scarab (from her dream)."

After that event, as Jung predicted, the woman became an excellent patient and worked on her problems. In his writing, Jung uses this story a perfect example of how synchronistic events can emerge from the paranormal world and impact peoples' lives.

39
An Exorcism?

The paranormal series of events that follow, again come directly from the book my wife Barbara and I wrote titled, *An Explosion of Being*. This is one of those things that happened along the way and left us shaking our heads. It is told from Barb's perspective:

"One of our more intriguing occurrences began when Doug came home after one of the many crisis days, during his ill-fated venture into business. His half-joking statement didn't make me laugh at all. 'Well, Barb, guess what? We've got our first exorcism.'

"'What!?' I was horrified. What a terrible prospect. 'You're kidding, right?' I was beginning to back out of the room.

"'Ah, well, yes, kind of, but ...' he stumbled. 'What I mean is that one of my associates at work has been seeing this, ah, well, ghost-like vision and I, ah, well, sort of promised we'd find out what it is.'

"As the story unfolded, it seemed that Doug had shared the concepts of his children's books with a woman in the office. This led to a discussion of afterlife and subsequently to a discussion of our book on the paranormal called, *An Explosion of Being*, including the trance communications portions.

"Doug's friend was fascinated. She proceeded to tell him about a ghostly image that kept presenting itself to both her and her daughter. Their request was simply to investigate, through our trance source, the nature of the sightings, nothing more.

"The request was simple, but its execution was not. Yes, Doug and I had seen images that might commonly be called ghosts, and, yes, our trance communications explained their appearances, but to actually investigate somebody else's haunting?

"Through Doug's gentle pressure and a few days of careful consideration, I agreed to give it a try. As long as Doug's friend understood that we guaranteed nothing, and the investigation would consist only of asking questions of our source, in our own home, then I would participate.

"With just Doug and me present, the writing session went perfectly, giving us a full page of information. Apparently, my nervousness left me entirely, as the words flowed of their own accord, in the usual manner. A little study showed some sort of cryptic reference to a spiritual guide that had always been with this woman.

"It seemed as if this continued appearance was meant to remind her of something that she needed to learn. On the surface, the words seemed logical, but we had trouble deciphering a completeness of meaning.

"The next day, Doug took the typed session to work, handed it to his friend, and explained what little we understood from the messages. Almost apologetically, he told her that the material may have no significance for her whatever, and to feel free to discard it if what was said didn't feel right. When his presentation was done, and after she had read the channeled material, she said, 'It may not make a lot of sense to you, Doug, but to me those messages are perfectly clear.'

"She went on to explain how, since childhood, she had seen a spiritual guide, such as the one mentioned in the Writings, but she had forgotten about it in recent years. She seemed very pleased with the content of what Doug gave her, allowing us both to breathe a sigh of relief.

"The matter would have ended there, except that a couple of weeks later, Doug happened to ask his friend how the ghost was faring. Her response was a startled revelation to herself. 'My God, we haven't seen it since you and I discussed the messages from your trance communications. It all made so much sense. Somehow, I didn't even realize that we weren't seeing it anymore.'

"And I hadn't wanted to participate in an exorcism? Hmm."

40
Goodreads and the
Skyway Bridge Story

Studying and writing about the paranormal as I do, tends to lead me into some very interesting experiences.

Often, those experiences are *coincidental* in nature, but so far above the possibility of randomness that they make me stand back in wonder. It's at those times I realize what I'm observing is something emanating from a source that demonstrates the unity of all things. Carl Jung used the term synchronicity to describe such linked happenings.

In his work, Jung validated the world of the paranormal and classified synchronous events as part of that world. If it's good enough for Jung, it's good enough for me.

A few years ago, I got a startling taste of Jung's synchronicity through a very unexpected source. During that entire month, as a promotional effort for my books, I offered to give away a limited number of copies on Goodreads, a website catering to millions of readers. One of those books was An Explosion of Being, the true-life story my wife Barb and I wrote about paranormal explorations.

The first edition of Explosion came out many years ago and in it, Barb and I did some psychic probing of a major Florida tragedy that occurred in those days called, The Skyway Bridge Disaster.

In a nasty storm, a ship struck a bridge south of here in St. Petersburg, Florida, destroying parts of it and sending thirty-five people to their deaths in the waters below. I say that glibly now but at the time, I felt anything but matter-of-fact. In addition to the sadness I felt at such horrible loss of life, my family and I had traveled on that bridge more than once. It could have been us.

OK, enough of that. Now, back to the Goodreads situation. As soon as the contest ended, the Goodreads people sent me the names of the winners and their addresses. Beforehand, I had purchased pre-stamped, Priority Mail envelopes. When I got those envelopes, I just glanced at them to make sure they were definitely pre-stamped, but that's as far as my inspection went.

Only about halfway into my stuffing those envelopes with books did I take a closer look at the stamp. Truly, I had to look twice before I would believe what I was seeing. There on the stamp was an artistic rendition of the new Skyway Bridge.

As if that wasn't enough synchronicity, I went online to see how long the stamp had been in service. Issue date, February 28, 2012, exactly one day before the start of the Goodreads contest. I must have *coincidentally* purchased my envelopes right around the time those stamps were being presented to the public in St. Petersburg.

I can just see Carl Jung nodding sagely and saying, "See! I told you so!"

41
The Ripley's Sequences

Here you have a very interesting mix of linked paranormal coincidences. It's a fascinating tale but complex to describe. Please bear with me as I set this thing up. I have put certain items in bold font to highlight them as reminders because each one of those are threads that help to create this intricate tapestry:

In 2011, I published Book I of **The St. Augustine Trilogy**, my paranormal/historical novel for young adults titled, *Sliding Beneath the Surface.*

The story mostly takes place in the **St. Augustine, FL neighborhood** called the Abbott Tract just north of the Castillo de San Marcos—the old Spanish fort.

Right at the edge of that neighborhood sits the original **Ripley's Believe it or Not Museum**. At night, Ripley's runs their **Ghost Train Adventure** that begins and ends there at the museum.

In *Sliding Beneath the Surface*, the main character, fifteen-year-old Jeff Golden, mentions he's been to **Ripley's** and there he saw a carved **Chinese puzzle ball** like the one Lobo, an old Native American shaman once handed to him. I had Jeff say all that because in my research travels to St. Augustine, I saw a large puzzle ball at Ripley's and decided to use it as a key paranormal symbol relating to the multiple layers of reality, hence it's appearance on the *Sliding* book cover.

In continuing first person comments, Jeff makes clear his dislike for all the tourists who flood St. Augustine and go on silly **ghost tours** like the one at **Ripley's**. Then Jeff describes times during terrifying paranormal exploits when he and his girlfriend, Carla:

- Encounter a soldier in front of the National Guard building

In writing *Sliding Beneath the Surface*, I mention in the book:

When I published the *Sliding* book in 2011, I also brought out a new edition of *An Explosion of Being* through my own publishing company. That book is dedicated to **my father** and describes his funeral at **West Point**.

It was Dad's death that started Barb and me on our investigations of the paranormal and resulted in the writing of *Explosion*.

Just after the first of this year, 2012, I contacted a friend of mine, Dave Lapham. Dave wrote two books on the ghosts of St. Augustine. I called him because I wondered how he had marketed his books.

Turns out, one thing Dave did was to set up **book signings** at Ripley's right there up the street from **the neighborhood** where all my fictional characters live. Dave suggested I gave Ripley's a call.

Ripley's? I had thought about book signings in St. Augustine but not at Ripley's. How interesting. Remember? Jeff in my young adult book mentions Ripley's and I got ideas for **The St. Augustine Trilogy** there.

At the time though, I was so swamped with other things that the thought of working St. Augustine book signings into my schedule just then seemed overwhelming. Dave's idea was a good one, but it took me until the week of May 14 to do anything about it. Here's where the coincidences really came flying at me. Yup, everything you've read up to this point has been prologue.

Early in that week, my friend Chuck Dowling, another author but a writer mostly of **military fiction**, emailed me.

He asked if I had ever thought of doing **book signings in St. Augustine.** I replied and said, yes, I had just put it on my calendar to call Ripley's on Friday based on Dave's suggestion.

A day or so later, I got an emailed newsletter from the **Seminole Wars Foundation** based in Bushnell, FL, of which I am a member. In doing research on the **Second Seminole War** for *Sliding*, I found the group's goals and activities very worthy.

Anyway, one particular article in the newsletter really caught my eye. The next meeting of the foundation was coming up and here's what it said, boiled down to the following bullet points:

The meeting will:

* Be held on August 18, 2012

I'm telling you what. I read that piece over several times, marveling at the fall meeting's connections with both my books and my father. To say all that was startling is to do it an injustice. I had yet to attend a meeting of the Foundation, but this one I could not miss.

For a few minutes, I just had to sit back and wonder how so many things could come together like that. Even believing at least some coincidences have significance, as is my thinking pattern, I was nowhere near prepared for such a rush of multiple, connected events. Synchronicity at its best. Carl Jung would have loved it.

Let's return to Ripley's now for a moment.

As planned on Friday, May 18, I called them. Ripley's that is. There I spoke to Ralf who was very receptive to the **book signing** idea. In fact, he said, it might be good for me to do one on a **Saturday** evening when there are a ton of their **Ghost Train** folks coming through the museum, and then again during the next day on Sunday.

After looking at my calendar and checking with my wife, the dates of July 14 and 15 were open for both of us and for Ralf so I immediately scheduled them. Perfect.

But that also got me to thinking. I would be going up to St. Augustine on **Saturday** August 18 for the Seminole Wars event during the day, right? That led me to ask Ralf about also doing another book signing that same night and then the following Sunday.

Again, both dates were open and I immediately scheduled them as well as those two days in July.

Actually, it was only after speaking with Ralf that the enormity of what I would experience on August 18 truly hit me. Wow.

With the **Seminole Wars event** during the day and **signing both books at Ripley's** that night, I had scheduled myself into living out all those coincidences within about an eighteen-hour span of time. And it had taken less than a week from the time my friend Chuck called asking me about **St. Augustine book signings** until I finally set everything up with Ralf. Quite a whirlwind of activity.

The universe had spoken and emphatically so, but why? Was there any purpose in all this happening in such a linked way, assuming it all fell together as planned? Was I just being guided somehow by a higher aspect of my own being? To be perfectly honest, I would like to think that it was some sort of confirmation of my efforts in writing and studying the paranormal. Maybe yes, maybe no.

But the universe is a tricky place, and when you try to interpret its intentions, it can very easily smack you upside the head. Some of those folks who study synchronicity suggest that intense coincidental events partially, at the very least, reflect your own thinking and observational patterns.

The idea is that you increasingly play a part in creating "coincidences" on a quantum level without realizing it. This can result in delusional cycles of self-reinforcement instead of revelation. Here is where people interpret series of coincidences that mirror their beliefs that the world will soon end and are just a bit disillusioned to find it hasn't gone away on schedule.

So, for now, I'm just going to be very thankful that I was privileged to watch such amazing patterns emerge out of our everyday world and fuse themselves into a structure in which I will be a grateful participant. No matter what, it's going to be fun to see it all unfold.

42
A Hummingbird and Stained Glass

This blog post of mine turned out to be only the start of a fascinating and intricately linked set of coincidental events. The story you will read below didn't end here because so much happened after I wrote it. See the next chapter for the continuation:

I think paranormal events sometimes occur when we think of people who are no longer in this life. Or, maybe it happens when they think of us. Anyway, in my mind, when such a thing occurs, it immediately connects me with the essence of that individual.

The exact reasons why this type of thing comes about isn't as important as the fact that, for me, it accomplishes something very important on an emotional and spiritual level.

One day, as I was writing at my desk, I took a stretch break and looked through the window on the other side of my computer. That always helps to refresh me since we have a large backyard full of trees and lush tropical growth. In scanning my little domain, I glanced at one of the pieces of my mom's stained glass art we had saved after her death. It is attached to the window and shows a hummingbird and a flower, and mirrors our backyard, since we have some flowers and the occasional hummingbird.

Mom had that same piece up in her kitchen window and I smiled with the memory of how much she enjoyed her house over on the coast at Indialantic, Florida.

As soon as that thought flashed through my mind, a hummingbird came out of nowhere and hovered just inches from the window.

Not only that, the position of its hovering was directly behind the stained glass hummingbird. The real creature was perfectly framed by the wire oval.

The little bird, with wings blurred in stationary flight, moved his head back and forth as if inspecting the interior of my home office. That lasted for about 10 seconds and then it was gone. The event couldn't have been scripted more perfectly.

Thanks Mom.

43
Infinite Hummingbird Connections

This chapter is the continuation of events from the previous page:

In my posts, I write a lot about how coincidences often show the true paranormal nature of the world in which we live. These events, especially when there are a series of them related to each other, can be a bit startling. Even so, over the years I've gotten fairly used to them. Once in a while, though, something will happen that really makes my jaw drop in wonder. That's what happened to me just a few minutes ago.

Let me back up here. Recently, I published a short article on my blog titled, "Paranormal Coincidences: The Hummingbird and Stained Glass." It was all about a set of simultaneous events involving a hummingbird right outside the window of my home office.

Today, I decided to post that piece on Facebook because it was a warm, touching story related to my deceased mother. In that article, I included a picture of a hummingbird and the stained glass.

Right after dinner, I checked my emails and noticed I had received a Google Alert. I have them set up so that Google scours the Internet for me on all kinds of subjects including, Doug Dillon and my book titles. Tonight, the Google email said, "Join Doug Dillon on Facebook."

Figuring it must be the hummingbird posting I did today, I clicked on it.

Sure enough, the hummingbird picture came up. The thing is, it wasn't *my* hummingbird. The color of the flowers was wrong. In fact, this picture filled a good chunk of the screen where my Facebook background photo actually showed the Bridge of Lions in St. Augustine at night. And my photo appears in front of that—a totally different set up.

Even so, the unfamiliar hummingbird picture still said, "Doug Dillon."

Finally, I tore my eyes away from the pictures and looked at the profile. That's when I discovered I was looking at a description of *another* Doug Dillon. That's what I said, another DOUG DILLON. Duh! Not only that, but this other Doug Dillon and I have these items in common:

- We both are retired

- We both are retired from a school system

- We are both retired from a school system in the state of Florida

- We both like history

- We both went to public universities in the state of Florida

See why I really stood up and took notice? As I looked at the other Doug Dillon's Facebook timeline, I saw this entire event as a giant cosmic exclamation point-one I will now have to insert into my original posting on the hummingbird and stained glass.

I immediately sent Doug # 2 a Friend Request. I think this event will blow his socks off. It will be interesting to talk to him.

UPDATE: The other Doug Dillon responded to me on Facebook where we are now friends. He read this article and found it pretty startling. This was especially true since he had some things to add to the string of *coincidences* listed above and here they are:

- Through his job back in those days, he once visited Orange County Public School's district office in Orlando where I worked. While there, he happened to walk by my office when he saw my desk with the Doug Dillon nameplate on it. Startled by seeing a name identical to his own, he stopped and asked if I was available. Unfortunately, I was away at a conference.

Doug and I think that we were destined to make contact no matter what. The thing is, it sure did take a long time. I would very much like to actually meet him one of these days.

44
The Issue of Slavery

I n my view, what you are about to read is much like strategically adding an exclamation mark to this book title as follows, Carl Jung, Hauntings and Paranormal Coincidences! Why? Because the events that you will soon read about occurred very recently and just a week before I was to submit the book manuscript for final formatting. It was as if these linked events rapidly fell into place as a parting salute to synchronicity and the connectivity between all things:

In my paranormal/historical young adult fiction series, **The St. Augustine Trilogy**, I have included both Native American and African American threads. In Book I, *Sliding Beneath the Surface*, Carla, a present-day African American teen, comes face-to-face with a Florida slave ancestor in the year 1835. In Book III, *Targeting Orion's Children*, the one I'm working on now, Carla and her boyfriend, Jeff, travel back in time again to Spanish St. Augustine, Florida in the year 1684. And in order for Carla and Jeff to accomplish their mission, they are forced to witness a horrific slave whipping in that city's plaza.

OK, the stage is now set for the series of fascinating coincidences that recently happened:

1. **An Instant Research Find:** Last week, I decided I needed more information on slave punishments in Spanish Florida. Usually, I bundle such questions

for a future visit to the St. Augustine Historical Society's Research Library.

On that day though, I felt an itch to initially see what I could find on the Internet about that subject. And when I entered the key words on Google, the *very first* source was a nonfiction book that included the description of an even more horrific slave beating than the one I was trying to create. Not only that, this event actually occurred in the *central plaza* of *St. Augustine, Florida*, just as I had planned, except it happened slightly over 100 years from my date of 1684.

As a matter of sad interest, the *female* slave who was beaten received *200* lashes and was forced to wear an *iron collar* for six years after that. How the poor woman even lived through such torture I will never know.

2. **An Invitation from the St. Augustine Historical Association:** As a member of SAHS, I often get invitations to various events sponsored by that organization. One such notice arrived by email about a month ago, but the topic for Monday September 22, 2014, didn't spur enough interest in me to travel the 100 miles from my home in the Orlando area.

    Last week, however, I received a corrected announcement saying the speaker planned for that event couldn't make it. In his place, the director of SAHS would give a talk about *slavery* relating to *St. Augustine.* Yes, that did make me sit up and take notice.

    And as a sidelight, coincidental situation, the

location of this presentation on slavery would be
given in historic *Flagler College*, the former Ponce
de Leon Hotel that opened in 1887. That site is
important because I use it as a major backdrop
for Book II of my trilogy tiled, *Stepping Off a
Cliff.*

3. **Monday, September 22, 2014**: Did I go to St. Augustine to hear that talk? You bet I did. In fact, I
invited a friend of mine, Gary, an old high school
buddy who lives in the city, to go with me. We
met for dinner beforehand and walked across *the
plaza* where that very nasty slave beating took
place in 1788. I actually use Gary's likeness to
describe one of my adult characters, Lyle, the
Homeless Guy, in the trilogy, and he has given me
permission to use a photo I took of him in all my
book trailers.

Tell you what, sitting there next to Gary A.K.A.,
Lyle, in *Flagler College* where a crucial aspect of
my *trilogy* takes places, and listening to a lecture
on *slavery* in *St. Augustine* after walking across
the same *plaza* where that nasty *beating* actually
took place in 1788, was quite an astounding experience. As far as synchronicity is concerned, it
couldn't get any better than that, right?

Wrong. Keep reading. Just one more event.

4. **Wednesday, September 24, 2014** (Today): This
morning, I planned on spending the entire day
working on Book III of the trilogy. But my wife,
Barb, called from where she works and asked me
to run an errand for her, which I did.

On the way home, however, I switched on the car

radio and listened to NPR as I often do. Turned out, the program was already in progress. The topic? A *novel* written for *young people* relating to the *African American* experience, including *slavery.* I never listen to the radio when I'm writing one of my books. And if Barb hadn't, just by coincidence, two days after my trip to St. Augustine, called and asked me to help her out, I would have never heard that program.

Yup, I came right home, put my novel aside, and immediately began writing this chapter. Sometimes, when the Universe rings, you just gotta put everything else on hold and take the call.

Section 6

Warnings, Predictions and Peeks into the Future

45
Jung: THE FLOOD

It was early fall in 1913 and Carl Jung had a definite feeling that something was about to happen. The feeling evolved into a deep sense of oppression that intensified daily.

In October of that year, during a trip he took alone, Jung had an hour-long vision that showed:

- A flood covering much of Europe

- The flood contained the debris from civilization

- There were bodies of drowned people everywhere

At the end of the vision, all of the water turned to blood.

Two weeks later, he had the same vision, only a more vivid version. At the same time, an inner voice told him that what he was seeing was real. Of course, as a psychiatrist, he was constantly analyzing himself through all this, but he also wondered if his vision might be precognitive in nature. If his vision was showing him something of the future, all Jung could conclude was that perhaps a revolution was coming to Europe.

No revolution occurred and Jung's visions subsided until the summer of 1914. At that time, he had another very intense dream in April that was repeated twice more, once in May and again in June. In this dream, he saw:

- Europe frozen over–snow everywhere with lakes, rivers and canals frozen solid

- Europe appeared deserted

- There was no green anywhere

The third time he had this dream, it ended with the understanding that the cold actual came from outer space.

At the end of July in 1914, Jung was invited to speak to the British Medical Association. The subject? "The Importance of the Unconscious in Psychotherapy."

On August 1, World War I broke out in Europe and immediately Jung realized what his dreams meant and that they had come from his unconscious. The timing of the topic for his speech to the British Medical Association, he felt, was simply an additional *synchronistic* event that showed how series of paranormal coincidences can lead to an understanding of ourselves and the world around us.

46
The Spider and the Lizard

Are all coincidences just random events? Are they sometimes happenings with connections that go well beyond those isolated occurrences?

My stance as forcefully stated in my young adult novel, *Sliding Beneath the Surface*, is that the events of our lives are tightly linked to each other in ways we will never fully understand. Every once in a while though, those linkages are so strong that they stand out like a road map. Here is an example:

I live in Florida with my wife Barbara, and we have more than our share of spiders. Of course, these spiders sometimes decide to join us *inside* our home and they can be fairly large. They are definitely unwanted guests. Even so, our response is to try and capture them, if possible, and give them another chance, *outside*.

Over the years we've gotten pretty adept at placing a drinking glass over each intruder, slipping a piece of cardboard under the glass, and then carrying glass, cardboard and spider out of the house.

One day we had a particularly large, hairy specimen crawl from behind a picture on the family room wall. Barb declined to capture it, and in no uncertain terms, delegated the job to me.

Dutiful husband that I am, the task was quickly accomplished. Once outside the front door of our house, I decided to release our unwanted guest on top of a large plant Barb keeps there.

I felt pretty good as I dumped the little critter on all that greenery, saving his life and all. Wishing him a long and happy existence, I turned to go back into the house when the plant started shaking. No spider could cause all that commotion.

The shaking stopped and when I bent down to inspect the plant more closely, I saw a very large lizard looking up at me with the spider in his mouth. In just a few gulps, the lizard downed the spider. So much for my intervention in trying to save the life of our hairy house guest, right?

Coincidence? Fate? Destiny?

It truly seemed that no matter what I did, my poor little old spider was not long for this world. The exact timing and the location of the critter's release almost seemed choreographed to end the spider's life and provide a meal for the lizard.

Beyond clearly pointing out to me the connectivity of all things, that sliver of life also dramatically showed me how little our human plans matter when other patterns of existence strongly lurk just around the corner.

47
Road Rage Incident

Premonitions can happen anytime. But when they occur as you're driving, they can be especially disconcerting. This short story is about once such incident:

I was on my way home after having visited a patient in my duties as a Hospice volunteer. As I scanned the four lanes of traffic around me, I suddenly had this vision of two guys fighting in the street in front of me. As soon as that picture flashed through my mind, I wondered why it had happened.

Almost immediately, I had at least a partial answer. A number of years before that event, I was driving on the same highway with Barb in the car. When we stopped for a traffic light, two men came out of nowhere, wrestling with each other and even bouncing off cars, including ours. My conclusion? Umm, maybe just being on the same road, perhaps at the same time of day, created the "fighting" vision. A weak conclusion, admittedly, but nothing else came to mind.

Seconds later, the traffic ahead of me thickened considerably. As it did, a black pickup truck swerved dangerously to the left, barely squeezing between two cars. The guy in the car now behind him slammed on his brakes and then swerved dangerously to his right, caught up with the truck in the lane to the right, and then matched speeds with it. The next thing I knew, both car and truck stopped dead in the middle of the highway. Luckily, I was in the far right lane, so I was able to zip past those two stopped vehicles without incident. But as I looked back in my mirror, car and truck were still unmoving as the drivers obviously raised hell with each other through their open windows. Traffic backed up behind them and people slowed to gawk—a dangerous situation all around.

Luckily, one or both of the drivers broke off their confrontation before it could escalate any further. Car and truck roared past me and out of sight, and I breathed a sigh of relief.

Had I been warned about that confrontation? If so, for what purpose? Was it just to show me how valid premonitions can be or was it something else? The only thing I can think of was that, after having the vision, I was highly vigilant in my driving. Maybe through such hyper-awareness, I was able to avoid having an accident.

48
The Hawk and the Tree

Sometimes the natural world speaks to us through paranormal means. All we have to do is listen and observe.

One day as I was writing on the computer, a hawk sitting high up in the huge oak in my back yard kept screeching. My desk and computer screen face the window so I could see him clearly.

The rear of our property borders the Little Wekiva River here in Central Florida, so it isn't unusual to see hawks, owls and all kinds of water birds. This time though, the hawk in question kept squawking his head off.

From his perch, he would look down on the ground below him, pause, screech some more and then look at me through the window. There was no question he could see me. Since it kept happening over and over again, it almost looked intentional, like he was trying to get my attention. *Nah, couldn't be*, I said to myself.

So I dismissed that notion, kept working, and eventually, my friend the hawk flew away. I figured he must have been eying a snake on the ground or something. A short time later though, he reappeared and repeated the same antics as before. "Crazy bird," I muttered, trying to finish the chapter I was writing.

Finally, I got hungry, went to the kitchen and grabbed some lunch right after my wife left the house to go somewhere. Just as I sat down to eat, I heard a heavy thud. At first, I thought the sound might somehow be her coming back in the front door but she didn't appear.

Curious, I called to her. No answer. I went to the front door and found it closed and locked. Now even more curious, I opened the door and saw that, indeed, her car was gone. That made me search the house, but there was nothing out of the ordinary.

Then on a hunch, I went back into my home office and looked through the window. The hawk was gone, but beneath our big old oak sat a huge mass of green about ten feet high where our back yard should have been. It took me a few seconds to realize I was looking at another tree that had fallen across the river into our backyard and onto our property. The thing had crushed our chain link fence and now lay exactly below where the hawk kept looking down and screeching.

Thankful I hadn't decided to work in the backyard just moments before, I wondered just what the hawk may have perceived so far in advance of what actually happened.

Interesting isn't it?

Update # 1: That event happened several years ago. I hadn't thought about it much until I selected this blog post for the book you are reading. And when I glanced over the text and the photo of a red-tailed hawk I used, that reminded me of how coincidental/synchronistic events tend to pop up more often when you are focusing them.

OK, fine, but I was really startled two days later while working out in my front yard. I had just about finished dumping a large bag of mulch around one of the several oaks that grow between our yard and our neighbor's home.

Just as I finished, I heard a loud thump just ahead of me. When I looked, there was a *red-tailed hawk* siting right on the edge of my neighbor's roof not ten feet from me. I figured the sound I heard was him landing on the roof and I was sure he would quickly fly off. Maybe he just hadn't seen me, was my logic. But no, he didn't move except for his head. He kept looking down, shifting his head from side-to-side to let each eye look at something on the ground. And when I followed his gaze, I saw a dead rat lying in my neighbor's grass.

Did the hawk accidently drop his kill onto my neighbors roof and that was the thump I heard, or was it the rat hitting the ground? Or maybe the thump was just the hawk hitting the roof at a high rate of speed. The answers to those questions aren't really important, but you can at least see my thought processes at the time. The thing is, that crazy hawk wouldn't move. Oh, he looked at me occasionally, but he was not about to give up his kill. Finally, after a couple of minutes, I moved a little and the hawk flew off.

Tell you what though, the coincidence of having such a close encounter with a red-tailed hawk like that right after reminding myself of that other hawk story, really made me stand up and take notice.

Update # 2: In keeping with how things often seem to flow with synchronous events and focusing on them, two weeks after inserting the first update to this story, I had another red-tailed hawk encounter. It was on my usual early morning walk around the neighborhood when I ran into another one of those large birds. Just like the one I saw recently, it was sitting on the edge of a roof and perhaps fifteen feet away from the sidewalk. He just stared at me imperiously, but made no move to fly away.

You know, I've been walking and driving in our neighborhood for thirty-eight years and the only times I've seen any kind of hawk on a roof like that were during the two times I've mentioned in these updates.

Does all this have any significance? Your guess is as good as mine. Perhaps such events speak to us on some sort of subconscious level or they are simply meant to remind us how connected we are to All That Is.

Update # 3: Here we go again. About a week after writing the above update, I had yet another red-tailed hawk incident just as it was starting to get dark. I was at my computer that faces our backyard. As is often the case, I was working on one of my paranormal, young adult fiction books when I happened to look up. There in our huge oak tree, was a raccoon. We have a lot of them running around and they especially like that tree.

The point though, is that just as I spotted the raccoon, a red-tailed hawk swooped in directly over the animal, as if he was trying to either catch him or knock him off his perch. I swear, the bird came within less than a foot of accomplishing whatever it was he wanted to do.

The question really is, why did I just happen to look up right at that second?

Anyway, the poor raccoon got so flustered he didn't know what to do. First he would start to go higher in the tree and then lower. Finally, he settled on going up, sheltering himself in leaf covered branches. During that time, the hawk flew back into the scene and perched on the branch of another tree near the oak. From there, he kept watch, I assumed for a reappearance of the raccoon

He sat there so long, I even called Barb in to see him. By then it was so dark that she could barely pick out his dark form against the slightly lighter background colors. The last I knew, before it became completely dark, he was still there. Owls hunt a lot at night, but I never heard of a hawk doing so. Then again, maybe my hawk education is lacking.

This is getting wild. We have lived in this house for almost four decades, as of this writing, and all of a sudden we have a huge flurry of hawk updates all within a short amount of time? If they were spaced over a number of years, or even decades, I could dismiss them. Not now though.

49
Broken Violin Strings

Back in 2009, my wife and I went to a concert at The Hard Rock Cafe here in the Orlando area. David Garrett, the great violinist was playing.

The guy is really terrific. He can shift from classical to rock and then into country in a matter of seconds.

In watching him though, my analytical mind started working overtime. Because the man moves that bow so incredibly fast, I wondered what temperatures his bowstrings reached with all that friction. Then I started wondering if he replaced those bowstrings before each concert to make sure they wouldn't break.

Not satisfied with those mental meanderings, I continued to wonder if his bowstrings broke very often during a concert and if that affected his performance greatly. Finally, I realized I wasn't enjoying the show because of all that internal questioning.

As a result, I made a very concerted effort to focus just on the music. Didn't happen. My obsession with the guy's bowstrings wouldn't leave me and, in fact, they strengthened. That really irritated me because I can usually let my thoughts go when I try, but not this time. The compulsion was really getting to me.

In tremendous frustration, I immediately started working diligently to refocus my mind. The thing is, less than two minutes after launching into that effort, Garrett actually broke several bowstrings. I couldn't believe it, but there they were just flailing away in the air as the guy continued to play. People all around me pointed and took pictures as Garrett courageously went on playing and finally ended that set with a flourish.

As soon as the music ended, he studied his broken bowstrings, fondled them a bit, looked at the audience, grinned, shrugged, and then went on playing. With all of my questions somewhat answered, I enjoyed the rest of the show and ignored the bowstrings still flopping in the air.

50
A Collapsing Dock

Have you ever been somewhere just at the right time when something happened? Later on, did you wonder how it was possible for you to be in that exact spot, at that precise instant? Just chance, some say, while others point to fate, destiny or God's will. Take your choice, right?

Well, for me, the longer I live, the more interconnected I feel to All That Is. In my view, those unseen linkages sometimes suddenly become apparent in such startling ways that I simply can't chalk it up to *coincidence.*

One such occurrence happened when I was visiting my mom at her home in the Melbourne, Florida area. This was shortly before her death in 2007.

We were sitting out by the pool in her back yard having a snack and chatting. After having taken a picture of mom with the canal behind her, I put my camera down, and for whatever reason, my gaze came to rest on the dock across the canal. In that photo, you can just barely make it out behind a palm tree to the left of where Mom sat.

As I looked, a woman came out of the house beyond the dock and walked out onto it. Just as she got to the end of the thing near a piling, that portion of the dock collapsed into the water. When the woman also fell into the water, I jumped to my feet, startling my mom. In that instant, I didn't know if that woman needed help, if I should dive into the canal to assist her, or what.

Seconds later, as mom turned to look where I was staring, the woman crawled out of the water up onto the badly tilted, and partially submerged, dock. Dripping wet, she scrambled to her feet and ran into her house. In the blink of an eye, it was all over.

"Oh my God," Mom said as she watched the woman climb out of the water and rush out of sight. As soon as I sat back down, with my heart racing, I told Mom how seconds before I "happened" to be looking in the exact direction of that event—right after having taken a picture of the scene where it would occur. We marveled at such a "coincidence" and I still do today.

My view at the time was that when we experience such things, it's simply an indicator that shows us the deeper, wiser portions of our selves. It's a little flag that says, "Hey you! Don't forget that under all that flesh, you are a spiritual being linked to everything in existence."

Beyond that though, we humans go wrong in two ways: (1) Ignoring such events and claiming they have no deeper meaning or (2) Trying to assign an immediate and definitive meaning to what happened.

Thinking about that event even more many years later, I now wonder if one or more of the following things could be true:

51
A Horrible Dream

This paranormal event is almost as difficult for me to share as it was when I wrote about it in *An Explosion of Being* many years ago. When my wife Barbara and I put that book together many years ago, we decided to include what you are about to read as a cautionary tale. I'm posting this experience for the same reason. The chapter from which it is taken is told from Barb's perspective, as you will see, but she quickly shifts to me telling my own story:

"From intriguing to unsettling is a big step, but this terrifying dream of Doug's and its conclusion in the physical world showed how quickly that transition can occur: 'Dream after dream shot their ways past me in rapid fire succession. They made a blizzard of random movements, people, objects and colors.

'Tossing and turning, I was physically and psychologically restless. Everything moved too quickly and nothing was understandable, until the motion slowed to a comprehensible focus on a small child. It seemed as if the child was a little girl, but I wasn't certain because she, or he, was running so fast.

'In a moment, the child's desperation was all too clear. Someone was in pursuit, and the child was fleeing in panic. The scenes then changed too rapidly to follow, until, once more, the focus was on the child, but this time he, or she, was sitting in a blue pickup truck. Again, the child tried to escape, but as the door opened, a slashing knife seemed to cut completely through the small body.

'Before I had time to react, the child was staggering through the woods, finally stopping just in front of me, critically wounded. Crouching in pain, the child looked at me, turning my growing revulsion into an agonizing desire to help. Reaching down, I gathered the youngster in my arms and held it close. In absolute horror, I realized that I was literally holding the child together.

'Lurching awake, I found myself trembling and in a cold sweat. Nicole, our three-year-old daughter must have sensed something. She had arisen, entered our room and was just standing by the bed, looking at me in the darkness. I reached out and hugged her, dissipating some of the dream's terror.

'The next day, I began a scheduled business trip along Florida's East Coast. On the way towards Jacksonville, a radio report, describing a child's abduction in south Florida seemed like just another bit of the world's negativity, so I paid little attention.

'After finally arriving at my destination and settling into the motel south of town, I went in search of a restaurant for dinner. But again, the radio blared news of that abduction. On it went, with the final chilling news that *part* of the child's body had just been discovered by search teams. My hands began to shake. Pictures from the horrifying dream the night before flooded my mind.

'Instantly, I knew that the dream action of holding a child together was symbolically valid. A part of me, I concluded, had spiritually stumbled into that event to help the child's consciousness repair the damage done through the pain and fear of that gruesome killing.

'Supper that night didn't settle very well. I left most of it still sitting on the plate and returned to the motel. Using the noise of television and the need to prepare for my meeting the next day, I was able to push thoughts of my dream and the child into the background. Sleep came much later, but only after wrestling with a piercing sadness and a raging anger at the injustice of physical life. I could still feel that trembling youngster in my arms.

'Incredibly, within the next couple of days, my original travel plans put me on a road passing the exact spot where the TV news reported authorities had found the abducted child's dismembered remains. That *coincidence* really jarred me. Expanded awareness can be a double-edged sword.'

"As Doug found out, this paranormal stuff can indeed cut two ways. On the one hand, it can clear a path for beautiful and satisfying perceptions, but on the other hand, it can reveal information that I suspect we might otherwise prefer to hide from our conscious minds. So called *psychic phenomena*, then, are perhaps just tiny bursts of recognition, both positive and negative, reminding us of the truer reality from which our physical existence springs."

One final note. The actual event I talk about during this experience was carried by national media outlets for a very long time. Even so, I didn't, and still don't, feel comfortable mentioning the names of the people involved. That experience was so real to me back then, it brought tears to my eyes when I told Barb about it. Still does.

52
The Breaker Box Entanglement

Should you pay attention when a *coincidence*, or coinciden*ces*, point to possible danger? And if you pay attention, what action(s) should you take, if any, to avert that danger?

My wife Barb and I are serious believers in the idea that everything in existence is connected and also linked to unseen worlds, dimensions, universes, etc., etc. This boils down to the understanding that no event is completely random, even though we may not understand how this comes about. For us, it's just something we accept as a demonstration of such connectivity and we don't have to prove causation to ourselves or anybody else. Nor do we question *why* something happened very much. Once in a great while, however, we are forced to look more closely.

Such a time came a couple of years ago when we got a letter from our electrician warning all his customers about the possibility of fire if they had a particular circuit breaker box made in the 1970's.

Since our house was built in 1976, we paid close attention.

Sure enough, we were the proud owners of one of the breaker boxes in question. That kind of shook me up because during the previous week I had *two* experiences with electrical fires: one at my chiropractor's office and one in a nursing home where I visit Hospice patients. Those fires were small and did little damage, but the fact that they both happened with me present, made me sit up and take notice. Besides, the stink of burning wires from each fire was still fresh in my memory, making the warning letter seem to glare at me from where I had placed it on my desk.

When I called the electrician, he said that during all those years since the '70s, the company did make some faulty breakers, but all-in-all, not too many fires occurred, and there had not been a general recall. His assessment was that a slight danger did exist but probably not much to worry about. He told me he felt obligated to send out the notice he himself had received, but since a new box would cost right around $1,000, it was highly questionable whether the minimal danger warranted such a high expense.

I liked what he had to say because I sure didn't want to shell out that kind of money unless it was truly needed. Still, I went on the Internet to research the situation myself. I came up with a mixed bag of results. The search verified much of what my electrician told me, but I also read reports by other electricians who said the breaker boxes in question were crap, they wouldn't have them in their homes, and they wouldn't install one. Not so good, but I *still* didn't want to pay $1,000 if I could help it.

Just as I had that thought about *not* paying the money, the power in the entire house flickered on and off. Woops. A power shift when I'm researching electrical problems and almost deciding to *not* get a new breaker box? Uh, that was a little too *coincidental* for comfort. As a result, I did another Google search and came up with a newsletter published by a civic association for the Village of Westover. Location? Very near Harrisburg, PA.

The entire front page was about the type of breaker box we had and how many of the homes in the community were originally constructed in the 1970's using identical equipment. Evidently, enough fires had begun because of those boxes that quite a few families in the Village of Westover purchased new equipment. One woman talked about how fire started in her home built in 1976—the same year mine was constructed.

After reading that woman's story, I happened to glance at the list of officers for the civic association from the Village of Westover. The last name for the immediate past president? *Dillon*, my last name. Not an overly common name. Yes, I did a double-take on that one.

In discussing this all with Barb, we decided there were just too many linkages to ignore. As much as we hated to do it, we reluctantly agreed to get a new breaker box installed. It didn't happen right away. I think it was a combination of my *still* not wanting to part with all that money and just being overly busy.

A couple of weeks later, while doing my usual walk around the neighborhood for exercise, I passed what was left of a house just up the street from us. For whatever reason, I had forgotten the thing burned up a year or two before. Since no repairs were made for so long, I guess I just accepted its looks as normal until that moment when the word *fire* suddenly sprang to mind. My neighborhood. 1970's. Oh my God!

After she arrived home from work that evening, I reminded Barb about the burned out house near us and my new reaction to it. Like me, she had put it out of her mind, but she immediately got on the Internet. After an extensive search, she found our city's report giving details about the house fire in question. In the document she read, it cited the cause as *faulty circuit breakers*. Within a week, we had a new breaker panel. Sometime you just gotta stop fighting the problem and go with the flow, right?

Update: May 23, 2012

A couple of months after having the new breaker box installed, our clothes dryer stopped working. So naturally, I called in repair guy. Turns out he had nothing to repair. He said I must have a faulty circuit breaker. What? No way.

Sure enough, he had me feel it and damn if the thing wasn't warm—a sure indication that a problem existed.

I immediately got the electrician back who installed our brand new breaker panel worth $1000. "Yup," he said, "that's weird. Shouldn't happen." He also said he didn't think it really put us in any danger, but he replaced the breaker section for no charge.

In retrospect though, what does this new information say about interpreting a series of coincidences and acting on them? All the original indicators pointed to danger, so we acted, right? But what if our interpretation was wrong? If there was indeed a message in all those coincidental events, it is conceivable this was it: by all means, *Do Not* buy a new breaker panel. It will contain a faulty part and *this* will put you in danger (the reverse of our original interpretation).

I bring this up to remind myself, and everyone else, how difficult it is to tease specific meaning out of coincidental events. This is one area where humanity has tripped itself up over the eons by assigning way too much meaning through the use of seers, oracles and psychics.

If the Multiple Universes Theory of quantum physics is correct, perhaps the strong indicators we see in a series of coincidental events may have a *probable* meaning, but it may have stronger or weaker shades of probability according to the universe in which you live. A huge caution sign.

Am I now second guessing our decision to install a new breaker box? I did for a few seconds, but as I weighed the two interpretations, I realized I would do the same thing again. Choices. It's all about choices but based upon as much cool analysis as possible.

Further Update: August 24, 2014

One more time. Since the last blog posting update on this story in 2012, we have had to replace yet *another* section of our NEW BREAKER PANEL. This time it was one hooked up to our air conditioner. Luckily, each time, those sections simply shutdown the power to those appliances and they were never a danger. Or so the electricians said each time. BUT those events do, again, speak to whether or not you should act on coincidental events in order to outguess fate, destiny, or karma. Unfortunately, though, the messages are not as clear as we might like them to be. And that makes actually doing something with such information a gamble.

What would you have done in our situation?

53
Jung: JUNG vs. FREUD

In 1909, Carl Jung visited Sigmund Freud in Vienna. Jung very much wanted his views on the paranormal, something that he, Jung, thought was very important. As they talked, it became apparent that Freud had no time for such far-out ideas.

The more Freud spoke, the more discouraged Jung became until he felt a very weird sensation in the area of his solar plexus. In fact, that region of his body actually became, as he called it, "tight and hot."

Just as Jung became aware of those sensations, a loud noise erupted from a bookcase standing very close to both men, startling them and making them jump. The noise was so loud, Jung thought the bookcase might fall on them, but it didn't.

Feeling certain that the noise had a paranormal origin, Jung told this to Freud. He tried to explain how what had just happened was just a sample of such events, but Freud would have none of it. When Freud continued to argue, Jung interrupted him and warned that another such noise was about to come from the bookshelf. Jung had no idea why he was so certain this would happen, but he felt compelled to make that prediction forcibly.

The second Jung finished speaking, another loud sound exploded from the bookcase. When that happened, Freud just stared at Jung in apparent amazement.

Jung and Freud never spoke about that incident again and their relationship cooled considerably. It was from this point on in their friendship, Jung believed, that Freud lost trust in him.

Section 7

Illness, Death and the Afterlife

54
Jung: THE SUICIDE

After giving a lecture, Carl Jung went back to his room at the hotel where he was staying.

Exhausted, he fell asleep until 2:00 AM when he suddenly awoke. In that rapid awakening, he felt a distinct wariness.

In fact, he was sure someone had entered the room. Obviously still alone, but not fully believing it, he even opened his door to look out in the hall. No one there either.

Still the sensation of someone being close by persisted until Jung felt a dull pain in his head. To him, it seemed as if something had hit his forehead and then went all the way to the back of his skull.

Even so, after tossing and turning for a while, he was able to sleep, but only to have his experience relived in a different way the next morning. That's when he received a telegram explaining how one of his patients had committed suicide. Sometime later, he found out that the man had shot himself in the head, the bullet entering the forehead and stopping at the back of the skull.

55
Greg's Illness

This experience again comes from *An Explosion of Being*, the book my wife Barbara and I wrote a number of years ago. It is an example of what I classify as an out-of-body event and it is told from my perspective:

"With Barb as the official family doctor, all those who are ailing come directly to her for help. Call it a culturally assigned role or attribute it to the history of Barb's medical family, but that's how it is in the Dillon household. Therefore, it was not at all unusual, when late one night, our son Greg (age 14 at the time) woke Barb with some sort of physical discomfort. Closing the door to our room behind her, she took Greg back to his room on the other side of the house for doctoring.

"Very, very vaguely, I remember the door closing, but within seconds, I was contentedly sawing wood. Then, in the deepest sleep, I could literally see and feel Greg standing beside the bed. He looked directly at me and said, "Dad, I need your help." Completely startled, I vaulted out of bed, half asleep. Barb was gone. It was dark. No Greg. The door was shut. What was going on?

"In sleepy confusion, I found Barb in Greg's room trying to ease his pain. He was in agony; excruciating headaches, vomiting-the works. When I walked in, they were both surprised. As with most teenagers, Greg usually liked to show old Dad how independent, detached and *together* he can be. It's a natural process, but on that night, minutes before I entered the room, Greg told Barb, 'Boy, I sure wish Dad was here.'

"When his symptoms began to ease, I explained my experience and asked Greg how he was able to awaken me all the way from his room. He laughed and shook his head, but for another hour, the three of us sat there and explored the possibilities together—not parents and child, but three people playing with ideas of mind and spirit.

"By this time in his life, through many such talks, Greg has come to understand much of his own potential. His conclusion about my dream was that it was an obvious telepathic linkage with him during his extreme pain. Sitting there listening to him hypothesize, I began to think about our daughter Nicole's nightly out-of-body travels. In both circumstances, without a doubt, I had been contacted as a helping agent in a time of crisis.

"On the surface, this was a very practical usage of nonphysical capabilities by both parent and children. Barb even complimented me on what she said would blossom fully one day into 'woman's intuition.' But, below the surface, both Barb and I definitely sensed that in all such experiences with our kids, they were the teachers, and we, the students."

56
Back from the Dead?

Near-death experiences often bring the paranormal world that permeates our existence home to us in very startling ways. There are a lot of stories about such circumstances, but one in particular has stayed with me for many years. Why? Because it was so startling and came from someone who witnessed it—a nurse.

I came by this testimonial when my stepdad lay dying in a Central Florida hospital. His passing was long and difficult. Family members were stretched to their physical and emotional limits. The medical staff was wonderful, doing their best to help us understand what was going on and making us comfortable.

At one point, the only people in the room besides my stepdad, a nurse and me, were my mother and my wife Barbara. We continually talked to my step dad, trying to ease his passage into the next world even though he was unconscious.

"Part of him knows you're there," the nurse said as she checked his vital signs yet once again.

"I guess you've seen a lot of this, huh?" I asked.

She looked at me, nodded and said, "Oh yeah. Too much of it if you want to know the truth. But then again, one case I had always sticks with me and gives me hope for us poor lost human beings."

I encouraged her to tell us about it and she did.

"Well," she said, "it was a night like this for another family. A young father had died and his family sat around his bed for a long time weeping and comforting each other. We let them stay as long as they wished. Every once in a while I would check on them to make sure they were OK.

"During one of those visits to the room is when it happened. Just as I walked in, the young man who had died sat straight up in bed with his eyes wide open. He looked at his wife who was holding his hand and said, 'I've been to the other side, but I've come back to tell you it's OK. All is as it should be. Please don't worry.'

"With that, he closed his eyes, collapsed and, well, died again. Permanently. I'm telling you, that man was clinically dead the first time. There was no doubt about it."

57
Jung: THE NEAR-DEATH
BREAKTHROUGH

In 1944, Carl Jung broke his foot. Not only that, he also had a devastating heart attack. Near death in a hospital, he proceeded to have visions that changed his life.

Those visions that came and went were so strong he knew he must be close to dying even though no one said this to him. His outlook got reinforced when a nurse told him she saw a bright glow all around his body.

At one point in his visions, Jung found himself high in space, looking down at the earth. Put simply, this is what he saw:

- The blue light of earth and the deep, rich colors of the land areas

- The continent of Asia below him

- Snow on top of the Himalaya Mountains

- The Arabian Peninsula

- Part of the Mediterranean

Remember, this was 1944, way before the age of orbiting space craft and artificial satellites. When Jung later asked a friend in the scientific community about what he saw, the friend told him that the only way anyone could actual see such things would be from 1000 miles in space.

Into Jung's vision appeared a gigantic, dark chunk of stone. As he stared at it, he noticed an entrance of sorts in the thing. Attracted to the entrance, he went through it and found a room where an Asian man dressed in white was meditating. There were little niches in the walls all around the room containing oil lamps.

As Jung approached the man, all sorts of strange things occurred:

- His entire earthly existence seemed to wash away as if the essence of who he was had been annihilated.

- Everything he had ever done, seen or planned left him completely. An extremely painful experience at first.

- Finally, as he realized he had been stripped of his identity, he also understood that he no longer needed, or wanted, anything at all.

- At that point, he accepted what was happening and realized the loss of his identity didn't matter.

Suddenly, Jung's awareness shifted and he found himself about to enter a huge temple. He knew without a doubt he would soon be meeting people inside the temple who had the answers to all of his questions. Finally, he would truly understand his existence.

Again, Jung had his awareness yanked in another direction before he could actually get inside the temple. Once again, he saw the earth far below him. But as he stared at it, he noticed something odd in the region of Europe.

Something seemed to be between him and that portion of the earth. Whatever the "something" was, it appeared to be getting bigger and coming towards him. And when "it" finally arrived, the object turned out to be the doctor who was treating Jung in the hospital. Immediately, Jung recognized the strength of his doctor's spirit that allowed him to make the journey all the way from earth.

Instantly, the doctor and Jung began to communicate—telepathically. The doctor told Jung that the earth had asked him to be its representative. This, the doctor said, was a protest against Jung's impending death.

As soon as the doctor delivered his message, the vision collapsed and Jung was back in his hospital bed and back to his very painful illness.

It took three weeks for Carl Jung to really make up his mind that he truly wanted to live. In fact, he initially developed an almost violent resistance to his doctor because Jung blamed the man for spiritually pulling him away from death's door.

When he was finally able to let that blame go, Jung started worrying about his doctor. He came to believe that the man's life was in danger because his spiritual trip up into space from Europe had drained so much of his life force.

After listening to Jung's description of the vision and the possible danger, the doctor dismissed it all as hallucinations. Angrily, Jung argued with the man, trying desperately to save his life. Those discussions went nowhere.

It turned out that Carl Jung was his doctor's last patient. Once Jung had fully decided to live, and was able to sit on the edge of his hospital bed, his doctor died.

According to Jung, the time after his illness (after 1944) was the most insightful and productive of his career. He died in 1961.

Author's Notes on The Book Cover

The Background Photo

My thanks go to NASA and the magnificent Hubble Telescope for this beautiful picture. I wanted to use it, not only for its attractiveness but also as something that would immediately capture the mind and send it on a journey into infinity even before the title is read.

This photo shows the Pinwheel Galaxy, M101. Its location is an inconceivable 21 million light years from our own Milky Way in the Ursa Major constellation. This object is 170,000 light years across and is about twice the size of our galaxy. Scientists believe that it consists of over one trillion stars.

The Green Bug

I love that big green bug. I put it in the forefront as symbolic of Carl Jung's Scarab Beetle experience. And to me, the juxtaposition of this very finite speck of life against the depths of such infinity in the background sets the stage for the book's content in a way that words never could.

Further Reading

Below, you will initially find some of the sources I used in uncovering information about Carl Jung and the topics of Coincidences and Synchronicity. The ones with an asterisk were the most helpful. The other books are excellent reads in a variety of fields, some of the ones that have led me to where I am now. Maybe you will find something in my listing that might spark your interest. I hope so.

On Jung, Coincidences and Synchronicity

1. *Jung, C. G. and Main, Roderick. *Jung on Synchronicity and the Paranormal*. Princeton: Princeton University Press. 1997

2. Jung, C. G. and Store, Anthony. *The Essential Jung*. Princeton: Princeton University Press. 2013

3. Kestler, Arthur. *The Roots of Coincidence*. New York: Random House.1972

4. *Surprise, Kirby. *Synchronicity: The Art of Coincidence, Choice and Unlocking Your Mind*. Pompton Plains. New Page Books. 2012

5. Wilcock, David. *The Synchronicity Key: The Hidden Intelligence Guiding the Universe and You*. New York. Dutton. 2014

Other Books Relating to the Paranormal, Spirituality and Related Scientific Discoveries

1. Alexander, Eben. *Proof of Heaven: A Neurosurgeon's Journey into the Afterlife.* New York: Simon & Schuster. 2012

2. Ajahn Chah. *Being Dharma: The Essence of the Buddha's Teachings.* Boston: Shambala. 2001.

3. Armstrong, Karen. *The Case for God.* New York: Alfred A. Knopf. 2009.

4. Berkowitz, Jacob. *The Stardust Revolution: The New Story of Our Origin in the Stars.* Amherst: Prometheus Books. 2012.

5. Burpo, Todd and Vincent,Lynn. *Heaven is for Real.* Peabody: Thomas Nelson. 2010

6. Chopra, Deepak. *How to Know God: The Soul's Journey into the Mystery of Mysteries.* New York: Harmony Books. 2000.

7. Dillard, Annie. *Pilgrim at Timker Creek.* New York: Perennial Classics. 1985.

8. Dillon, Barbara and Dillon, Douglas. *An Explosion of Being: An American Family's Journey into the Psychic.* Altamonte Springs: Old St. Augustine Publications. 2011. (The first edition was published by Parker Publishing, an imprint of Prentice Hall in 1984)

9. Edward, John. *Afterlife: Answers from the Other Side.* New York. Sterling Ethos. 2010.

10. Gleick, James. *Chaos: Making a New Science.* New York: Penguin Books. 1987.

11. Goswami, Amit. *The Self Aware Universe: How Consciousness Creates the Material World.* New York: Tarcher. 1995.

12. Greene, Brian. *The Elegant Universe: Superstrings, Hidden Dimensions, and the Quest for the Ultimate Theory.* New York: Vintage Books. 2003.

13. Guthrie, John. *Cassadaga: The South's Oldest Spiritualist Community.* Gainesville. University Press of Florida. 2000.

14. Hawking, Stephen. *A Brief History of Time.* New York: Bantam. 1998.

15. Kaku, Michio. *Parallel Worlds: A Journey Through Creation, Higher Dimensions, and the Future of the Cosmos.* New York: Anchor Books. 2006

16. Lama Surya Das. *Awakening the Buddha Within: Tibetan Wisdom for the World.* New York: Broadway Books. 1997.

17. Lapham, David. *Ghosts of St. Augustine.* Sarasota. Pineapple Press. 1997

18. _____. *Ancient City Hauntings.* Sarasota Pineapple Press. 2004

19. _____ *Ghost Hunting Florida.* Clerisy Press. 2010

20. Moody, Raymond. *Life After Life.* New York: Bantam. 1976

21. _____. *Reflections on Life After Life.* New York: Bantam/Mockingbird. 1977

22. Neal, Mary. To Heaven and Back: *A Doctor's Extraordinary Account of Her Death, Heaven, Angels and Life Again: A True Story.* Colorado Springs: Waterbrook Press. 2012

23. Roberts, Jane. *The Individual and the Nature of Mass Events: A Seth Book*: Englewood Cliffs: Prentice Hall. 1974

24. _____. *The Seth Material.* Englewood Cliffs: Prentice Hall. 1970.

25. _____. *Seth Speaks*. Englewood Cliffs: Prentice Hall. 1972

26. Ross, Diane. *Meditations for Miracles: The Keys to Life Mastery*. Orlando. 2010.

27. Seif, Charles. *Decoding the Past: How the New Science of Information is Explaining Everything in the Cosmos, From Our Brains to Black Holes*. New York: Viking. 2006

28. Sogyal Rinpoche, Gaffney, Patrick, Harvey, Andrew. *The Tibetan Book of the Living and Dying*. San Francisco: Harper. 2012.

29. Steinhardt, Paul and Turok, Neil. *Endless Universe: Beyond the Big Bang-Rewriting Cosmic History*. New York: Broadway Books. 2007.

30. Targ, Russell. *The Reality of ESP*. Wheaton. Theosophical Publishing House. 2012.

31. Thich Nhat Hanh and Kotler, Arnold. *Peace is Every Step: The Path of Mindulness in Everyday Life*. New York: Bantan. 1992.

32. Tucker, Jim. *Life Before Life: A Scientific Investigation of Children's Memories of Past Lives*. New York. St. Martin's Griffin. 2008.

33. Wambach, Helen. *Life Before Life*. New York: Bantam. 1979

34. Weiss, Brian. *Many Lives, Many Masters: The True Story of a Prominent Psychiatrist, His Young Patient, and the Past-Life Therapy That Changed Both Their Lives*. New York: Fireside Books. 1988.

35. Wolf, Fred. *The Dreaming Universe. A Mind Expanding Journey into the Realm Where Psyche and Physics Meet*. New York: Simon & Schuster. 1994.

36. Wright, Robert. *The Evolution of God*. New York: Little Brown. 2009.

37. Young, Samuel. *Psychic Children*. New York: Pocket Books. 1977.

38. Zukov, Gary. *The Dancing Wu Li Masters: An Overview of the New Physics*. New York: HarperOne. 2009.

Special Acknowledgements

Diane L. Ross
www.dianeross.com

What a pleasure it is to have Diane do the forward for this book. I am truly honored. Her kindness, wisdom, expertise and insights are, and always have been, an inspiration for me. Her own book, *Meditations for Miracles*, is a wonderful volume, jammed full of deep understandings and compassionate guidance. The only things more enjoyable than reading her words are to either speak with her personally or have the privilege of sharing a stage with her as I have on more than one occasion.

Dave Lapham
www.davelapham.com

Dave did the groundbreaking onsite research that first told the true ghost stories of St. Augustine, Florida:
- Ghosts of St. Augustine and
- Ancient Hauntings: More Ghost Stories from St. Augustine

It was his efforts in that arena that helped give birth to all the many ghost tours that are now available in that city, the oldest and most haunted in the United States. Dave's work helped me to lay a basis for my paranormal young adult trilogy as well as to populate my blog and this book with his writing. When we do presentations together, there is a natural flow between us that is a pleasure to experience every time it happens.

Mary Jo Fister and Greg Bush
Offthetrails Paranormal Investigations (OPI)
http://www.offthetrails.com/paranormal-investigations/

This delightful husband and wife team are my *go to* friends in the area of professional ghost hunting. My first official ghost hunt was with them and chronicled within this book in Chapter 13, "Ghost Hunting in a Bookstore."

What a pleasure and an education it was to participate with them as they probed deeply into physical manifestations of the spirit. These good folks have also allowed me full access to their field reports for use in my blog and in this book. And when we do presentations together, people flock to them afterward so they can see all that intriguing equipment and learn how it all works.

Patrick Delsaut
http://patrick.delsaut.perso.neuf.fr/presence_dautres_
mondes_menu.html

My friend, Patrick is a biochemist, researcher and writer about all things paranormal who lives in France. He is a delightful person, immensely intelligent and very passionate about uncovering the mysteries of existence. He has generously shared some of his own paranormal experiences with me for my blog and this book. And when he finishes translating his books from French to English, I will be among the first in the United States to eagerly devour them. Check out his website above. He has a translator hooked up so you can view it in whatever language you wish.

About the Author

Doug Dillon is a former educator who authors fiction and nonfiction for both young people and adults. He has written for *Boys Life* magazine, *The Orlando Sentinel*, The Florida Council on Compulsive Gambling, Harcourt, Mitchell Lane Publishing and Old St. Augustine Publications, to name a few.

Doug and his wife Barbara entered the literary field many years ago when they shared their own paranormal experiences with the world in their book, *An Explosion of Being: An American Family's Journey into the Psychic,* published originally by Parker Publishing, in those days, an imprint of Prentice Hall. During that first year of media exposure, Doug and Barb participated in many interviews and call-in radio shows not only across Florida but across the United States and up into Canada.

Doug is also the author of **The St. Augustine Trilogy**, an historical/ paranormal/ science fiction series for young adults, and adults young at heart, set in contemporary St. Augustine, Florida, the oldest and most haunted city in the United States.

Doug invites you to visit him on his website at
www.dougdillon.com

Index